THE SALINAS

Upside-down River

THE
RIVERS OF AMERICA

Edited by
HERVEY ALLEN

As Planned and Started by
CONSTANCE LINDSAY SKINNER

Art Editor
RUTH E. ANDERSON

THE SALINAS

Upside-down River

by

ANNE B. FISHER

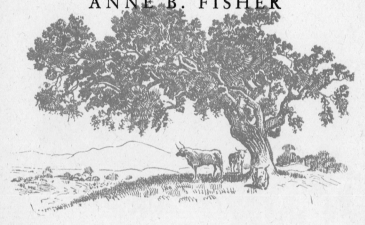

Illustrated by
WALTER K. FISHER
FARRAR & RINEHART
INCORPORATED

New York   *Toronto*

This book has been manufactured in
accordance with the paper conservation
orders of the War Production Board.

To all who long to know about the country in which they live and who don't want to go to sleep reading about it.

Contents

PART VIII. "BLUE BELLIED BLACK REPUBLICANS
AND DEMOCRATICAL HYPOCRITICAL
SECESSIONISTS"

PART IX. DROUGHT

PART X. DEER, ANTELOPE AND CLOSE
VOTES. 1872

PART XIII. GREEN GOLD AND TROUBLE

PART XIV. TRUCKS IN THE SILENT NIGHT

Prologue

GEOGRAPHERS are cold fellows. They tell us that the Salinas of California is the third longest river in the state and the largest submerged stream in America; that its source is in the mountains east of San Luis Obispo, just about one-third of the way between Los Angeles and San Francisco, and that as the crow flies it is only about twenty-five miles from the treacherous coast of the Pacific.

The principal tributaries of the Salinas are: Estrella River, which forms the source and rises in the mountains which divide the Salinas from valleys draining to the south; the Nacimiento (Birth of Christ) and San Antonio rivers, both of which rise in the Santa Lucias and flow southeast parallel to each other for thirty miles to empty into the Salinas north of Mission San Miguel, which is about one-fifth of the way down the valley; the San Lorenzo which flows southwest from the Gabilans on the east side of the valley to join the Salinas near King City; the Arroyo Seco, which rises in the Santa Lucias and flows northeast into the Salinas south of Soledad, which is two-thirds of the way down the valley.

The Salinas River valley proper is a comparatively narrow trough extending from northwest to southeast between the dry Gabilan (Hawk) Range on the east and the moister and far more rugged Santa Lucias on the west. But from high up on the pass to the south near its head the Valley appears as a great plain from ten to twenty miles wide cut up by side valleys into hundreds of rounded grass-covered hills from two to four hundred feet high, their summits almost the same height, so that there is a feeling of vast distances.

The Santa Lucia range rises abruptly from the Pacific without benefit of coastal plain or foothills. Some of its hundreds of sharp ridges and peaks exceed 5,000 feet. Along its valley flanks there are foothills with chaparral and oaks, or under grazing.

The Gabilan range on the east side, which divides the Salinas from the interior valleys, is billowed with bare hills that are green in winter and spring and tawny in summer.

The Salinas valley lies parallel to the coast and the river flows 150 miles northwest into Monterey Bay. The valley has about 640,000 acres of broad wide bottom land, and is fifteen miles wide on the plain near its mouth. One of the most productive valleys in the United States, it is often called, "The Valley of the Nile."

All this those matter-of-fact fellows the geographers tell us, but with the geologists the story of scene-shifting in the Salinas is a wondrous one. The present vista of valley and mountains is recent, the details having been sculptured from sedimentary rocks of the middle and late Tertiary, although the core of the Gabilans and Santa Lucias is much older, having supplied some of the materials of these later rocks.

We can hark back with some confidence to the Jurassic (perhaps 175,000 millenniums ago) when there seems to have been a narrow granite and probably mountainous land mass in place of the Salinas Valley, extending northwestward into the present Pacific. On the east was a wedge-shaped gulf covering northwestern California, its head being southeast of Paso Robles. On the west, the Pacific received from the mountains of this old "Salinia-land" a great thickness of sediments, later consolidated as the Franciscan series which forms the bulk of the southern Santa Lucia Mountains.

During the 87,000 millenniums of the Cretaceous period much of the old narrow Salinia-land persisted, its mountains worn low from contributions to the "Santa Lucia sea" and to the great gulf that covered much of northwestern California west of the recently formed Sierra Nevada. In some localities in California sections of sandstone attributed to the Cretaceous attain the almost unbelievable thickness of 25,000 feet, eloquent testimony to the time involved in their deposition.

Salinia was a very old land when the Rocky Mountains arose toward the end of the Cretaceous period, which saw the culmination of the great reptiles and the evolution of the true birds and first flowering plants. Salinia was so old that it must have been worn to a plain.

During the ensuing 90,000 millenniums of the Tertiary age, *some* part of it was always under the sea, and during the Upper Miocene period not only was the entire valley covered, but most of central California as well, including regions which are now ruggedly mountainous. During Lower and again during Upper Miocene (over a period of 20,000 to 25,000 millenniums) there was in many places extensive volcanic activity, to which California and Nevada owe much of their wealth in gold, silver and other metals. In the seas of California thousands of feet of shale were deposited, including a large proportion of material suited to be the source rock of petroleum.

The Quarternary (or Pleistocene), following the long Tertiary age, although short in comparison (2,000 millenniums) witnessed the formation of the Santa Lucia and Gabilan mountains which were then probably several thousand feet higher. Extensive erosion roughed out the modern features of the mountains and contributed deep deposits of silt in the northern part of the valley. Drainage from the Salinas and the great interior valley of California emptied into Monterey Bay and scoured out a deep canyon which can now be traced seaward to a depth of more than 6,000 feet. This was followed by a long period of gradual depression when the lower Salinas Valley was again flooded. In the meantime separated periods of heavy precipitation and lowered temperature brought on severe glaciation in the Sierra Nevada Mountains as well as elsewhere in the Northern Hemisphere. There is no evidence of glaciation in the Santa Lucia Mountains, but everywhere the deep canyons and intricately sculptured ridges point to much bad weather, when roaring torrents transported some of the mountains to bury deep under the Salinas River the backbone of the old Salinia.

Finally, a period of uplift established the modern coast line and details of modern scenery. Soon afterward the most ancient Americans moved in.

Little is known of these ancient ones who came to live in the Salinas and leave behind them only strange hieroglyphics on the walls of caves high above the floor of the valley.

Then again the rich and fertile valley of the Salinas sent forth her challenge:

> "Bring me men to match my mountains
> Bring me men to match my plains
> Men with empires in their purpose
> And New Eras in their brains."

And so to the Salinas and the men who conquered her and prospered.

PART I

Beginnings

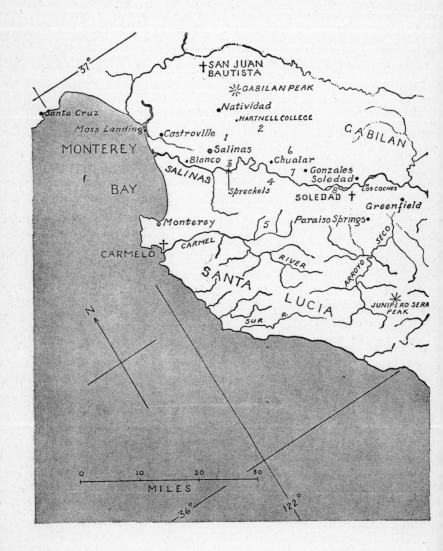

SAN JUAN
BAUTISTA

✳GABILAN PEAK

•Natividad
•HARTNELL COLLEGE

GABILAN

Santa Cruz
Moss Landing
•Castroville   1
                2
MONTEREY   ◎Salinas
        •Blanco   3   •Chualar   6
BAY   SALINAS   7 •Gonzales
                    4   Soledad•
        Spreckels   LOS COCHES
                        SOLEDAD 8 †
        ◎Monterey   Greenfield

CARMELO †   5   •Paraiso Springs
        CARMEL

        SANTA   RIVER   SECO

                LUCIA   ARROYO

N   SUR   R.   JUNIPERO SERA
                            PEAK

0   10   20   30
            MILES

37°

36°   122°

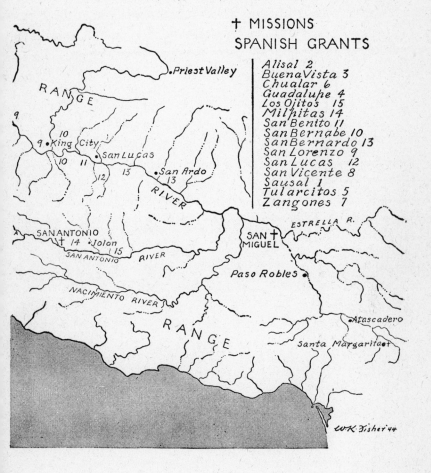

SALINAS RIVER · CALIFORNIA.

✝ MISSIONS

SPANISH GRANTS

Alisal 2
Buena Vista 3
Chualar 6
Guadalupe 4
Los Ojitos 15
Milpitas 14
San Benito 11
San Bernabe 10
San Bernardo 13
San Lorenzo 9
San Lucas 12
San Vicente 8
Sausal 1
Tularcitos 5
Zangones 7

Priest Valley

RANGE

9

10
9 · King City
10   11   · San Lucas
    12   13   · San Ardo
              13

RIVER

SAN ANTONIO
✝ 14 · Jolon   · 15
SAN ANTONIO   RIVER

ESTRELLA R.

SAN ✝
MIGUEL

Paso Robles ·

NACIMIENTO RIVER

RANGE

· Atascadero

Santa Margarita ✝

W.K. Fisher '44

I

1769

Hot september sun and an expanse of clear blue sky overhead; below, a great wide plain, a trackless golden wilderness of waving grasses with heads bent hard to south in the constant wind—toward the south where weary Spanish explorers rested after their steep climb over the cruel pass. Portola and his men had arrived! The first white men looked out across the great valley of the Salinas, with its green ribbon of cottonwoods that marked a river. They looked upon the valley that was to welcome adventurers of all nations, to prosper most of them, to bring sorrow and greed to others, murder to some, and then to lie ever golden and smiling like a confident courtesan ready to ensnare still more men with her rich promise.

They were a footsore discouraged lot, these soldiers and scouts from New Spain, who chopped their way through brush with long knives, and who cried out and lashed rawhide thongs at the small heavily burdened pack horses. The way had been long and tedious, with only the tall peaks of the Santa Lucias standing high up to guide them; Santa Lucias, the sentinel mountains that had for more than two centuries guided galleons on their way from New Spain to the Philippines, Sandwiches, and the Orient; Santa Lucias, landmark mountains of Cabrillo and Vizcaíno, that prom-

ised wilderness wanderers the bay named after the Count de
Monterey; Santa Lucias, devil mountains, no saint about
them, moving the bay ever farther away with each day's
march. The soldiers were weary of them and the promise of
what was to come.

Until now the tale all the way from San Diego had been
no water except stinking little springs befouled by wild
things who had come first, food lowering in packs with each
setting sun, and so many mouths to feed that were of no
help. Still no sign of the much-sought bay.

They pushed along this strange river that would be up
to the horses' bellies sometimes, and would then go underground for miles. The river was a trap of quicksand in places.
Several horses and their precious packs were sucked out of
sight before they could be rescued. There was plenty of
grumbling and muttering as they made camp in willows
that grew beside the niggardly autumn-sapped waterway.

The Franciscan padre who had come along to take care
of the adventurers' morals and souls, if need be, and to
attend God's interest in this new venture to gain more lands
for New Spain, was eager to call the river at their camping
place El Rio Eleazerio, after St. Eleazer. Disgrunted soldiers
only sniffed and suggested El Rio del Chocolate, after the
delectable luxury they could no longer have. At least it
looked like chocolate when stirred up.

Officers and religious ones compromised and called the
stream Rio Santa Delfina. Water, no matter how muddy,
must be gratefully received and the saints had need to know
that their worldly children had not forgotten them in this
vast wilderness where water was so scarce. If thanks be
shown for what was received, reward of better water might
come, should courage march along with faith.

The padre's miracle of faith worked! After the next
day's march to the west they reached a broad side valley
where a clear cold stream bubbled through a canyon as if

it would deny the time of year and make only a bad dream out of the golden heat-seared hills and lack of rain.

There was manna in the wilderness too. Indians, coming down from their mountain place of worship where men beyond history had painted a cave with symbols in red and black and white, saw these new creatures with long knives and strange four-footed beasts to carry burdens.

These new men were not like themselves, except some dark-faced ones who carried packs. But even these were not dressed in skins or rushes. They were hampered at every step by much covering of the body. No wonder they were all so weary that they stumbled along heavy-footed and drooped of shoulder. Who would want to wrap up arms and legs this way and bring sweat to the face?

The curious Indians came nearer and found these new men friendly; they offered pine nuts from the recent harvest and meal made from acorns, and held out hands to receive beautiful beads, the like of which had never been seen before. And so it was that soldiers and scouts and geographer, priests and officers of Portola had their fill of clear water and their bellies temporarily eased by food from the hands of those they called savages.

When strength came back into half-starved bodies the march to the sea pushed on, for now nights were growing bitter cold, and snow had fallen on the high peaks to the west. In spite of help from friendly Indians, the food was too low to last long or even think about with any comfort. They *must* find the bay of Monterey.

But Portola, the brave Spanish explorer, reckoned not with vast spaces. The clear atmosphere brought things nearer than they were and deceived the senses. Famine was ahead. They had to kill the weakest of the mules to eat, and this without even salt to make the tough scaly flesh more palatable. There were losses in soldiers so that the padre was busy praying for the sick and attending the souls of those who would leave their bones in this valley of winds.

Fear conquered. In December, 1769, Portola and his men retreated, this time with their backs to the wind. Weary and discouraged they passed below the caves where prehistoric men had left their hieroglyphics of horses and strange beasts, climbed the steep grade, and went out of the land where they had hoped to find the sea.

The valley of the river Santa Delfina, later to be called Rio Monterey and still later the Salinas, had won the first battle against those who would conquer her and slept once more in golden peace.

No Defeat

Portola was not a Spaniard to take defeat. Back at San Diego once more he talked long with the missionary Padre Junípero Serra and with Miguel Costansa, his own geographer, engineer and mapmaker. Spring was the time to make the trip in search of Monterey Bay; smaller party, too, so that enough food could be carried. He called for volunteers among the Catalans of newly founded San Diego to go along with soldiers of the garrison and their officer Don Pedro Fages. There were to be twenty in all.

New shoots of April green pricked up through the golden ghosts of last year's grasses when the second party reached the plain of the Santa Delfina. Willows where they had camped before were awash with deep swift-flowing water; the river had spread so that in some places it was two miles wide where formerly they had jumped across it. One cautious realist in the party, thinking of that other defeat suffered only a few months before and full of fear because Constansa the mapmaker was not long, reached into a pocket where he had concealed a bag of mustard seed. As he went along he dropped a few seeds. Mustard would grow fast and bloom quick as a miracle. The party could retrace their steps again if need be, guided by golden blooms of mustard. They would be thankful for this foresight.

Indians in the side canyon again greeted them with

eager eyes and hands out for more beads. They recognized a young soldier who had come before, José Maria Soberanes.

Now there was no need to rest half-starved bodies and there was the added excitement of meeting at Monterey, Padre Junípero Serra and Don Miguel Costansa, who had sailed on the packet *San Antonio*. Spring with its lush green growing season entered the very blood. They must push on to the sea.

Victory came to the travelers by land, for they struggled through the salt marshes at the mouth of the river and reached Monterey Bay on May 23rd, while those who traveled in the dancing little packet tossed about on the waves until the 31st. This victory must have been a bit hollow to some in the party, for they found that the disheartened Portola had formerly camped within a day's march of the bay which General Vizcaíno had discovered one hundred and sixty-eight years before and named for the Count de Monterey, the viceroy who had sent him from Mexico.

They changed the Santa Delfina to Rio Monterey, and then to the Salinas, because of the salt marshes at the mouth where flocks of great white herons fished for their supper in the pink glow of evening.

Portola told Padre Junípero Serra about the Indians living near the side stream that was clear and plentiful even in dry September and December. Eagerness lighted the padre's eye, and zeal for the conversion of gentiles burned ever hotly in the old missionary's heart. As soon as the Mission of San Carlos de Borromeo was established in Monterey and the land along the Rio Carmelo explored, he would go himself to those Indian children who waited to hear of God. Never again was the wide plain of the Salinas to sleep peacefully in waving green or gold, with only Indians to hunt antelope among her hills and fish in her tributaries.

3
Padres

HOT JULY sun sweated the very life juices from the little band of missionaries, as they trekked on foot southeast from the coast and through a low rocky pass in the Santa Lucias. Loose stones worked wickedly between bare feet and sandals, and eyes must be ever alert for rattlesnakes on the path, so they missed the flaming beauty of scarlet trumpet flowers and yellow brodiæas on the hillsides. Brown robes brushed against gray sagebrush and the bruised shrub filled the nostrils of the newcomers with its pungent fragrance.

There were three padres, led by Junípero Serra, the presidente of the missions, a few soldiers for protection, and last of all, mules carrying the necessary equipment for the new mission that would be built beside a tributary of the Salinas.

Once over the pass they came upon a large canyon thickly forested with oaks, which they named Los Robles, and there they set up camp. Costansa's maps were accurate. There was the wide plain and the stream fresh and cold in spite of July sun. Here was water to irrigate the crops they would put in. The good God was blessing them. The river would be called San Antonio of Padua after the Franciscan monk and saint they all adored.

Serra took possession, ordered the mules unloaded and

bells hung up on an oak limb. For this bringing of God into the wilderness, royalty of Spain and pious ones in both Spain and Mexico had given a fund of five million dollars. Here now in the Salinas would those generous ones be blessed.

PADRE JUNIPERO SERRA

When all was in readiness the humble Serra himself began to tug at the first bells ever to ring through the silent valley.

"Hear, oh gentiles," he shouted joyously. "Come, oh, come to the Holy Church! Come to receive the faith of Jesus Christ!"

A less zealous and more realistic priest watched for

a bit, then begged Serra to save his energy. "Why do you weary yourself unnecessarily? This is not the place where the church will stand, nor is there anywhere within hearing in these regions a single pious soul. It is of no use to ring the bells."

To this Serra answered: "In this way let me give expansion to my heart, as I would that this bell might be heard in all the world, or at least by all the pagan people who live in this sierra."

The cross was set up and blessed. A little shelter of branches was made and under it the first Mass said in honor of San Antonio, the patron saint of the mission to be.

A single Indian, attracted by the ringing of the bell, came near and was a witness. This the venerable Serra discovered as he turned from the altar to preach the sermon after reading of the Gospel. Heart overflowing with joy he cried out: "I trust in God and the favor of San Antonio that this mission will come to be a great settlement of many Christians, because what we see here has not been seen in any other mission founded. At the very first Mass, the first fruits of paganism have been present. He will surely not fail to communicate to his fellows what he has seen."

The padre made little gifts to the savage in order to attract others, and before nightfall spread its dark blanket over the weary travelers that July 14, 1771, many curious Indians had come to the newly founded Mission San Antonio.

God was in the valley of the Salinas.

4

Famine

Pagan indians the next morning watched padres say
Mass and heard them sing the Canticle of Dawn, as they
faced east with hands outstretched toward where the sun
would rise. Liquid Spanish rang out through the crisp morning air.

> Now comes the dawn
> Brightening to the day
> Hail, Mary, Hail
> Let us all say.
>
> Born was Mary
> For Heaven's light
> And help of sinners
> In their plight.
>
> Alone in beauty
> Unequalled one
> Mary, thou comest
> Fair as the sun.
>
> Comes morning light
> Brightening the day
> Amen Jesus
> Let us all say.

Shortly after sunrise the first fence in the valley of
the Salinas was started to enclose the little compound where

God, two padres, and a corporal's guard were to make their habitation.

Junípero Serra, ever anxious for the establishing of more missions, was soon off along the trail, and those left went about building shelters for padres and soldiers, as well as erecting a makeshift place of worship to serve until the mission could be started. Enthusiasm for this new project in the wilderness captured the imagination of the six soldiers and three mariners who had been sent as guard. The corporal himself was interested in making a go of things and worked hard as any padre in bringing trees down from the near-by hills to fashion a barracks.

As time went on, building had to be stopped every few days in order to cultivate a little land. There were so few to work and teaching pagans by sign language and symbols was slow to bring results. These children of nature had never tilled the soil and it was hard to make them understand that corn must be planted and left in the ground if there was to be enough for all. Those childlike ones went out by night and dug up what had been planted during the day, sifted out the dirt through a crude willow sieve they had made, ate some of the precious corn and hid some. This hidden treasure took time to find, then the planting started all over again, until, after eight or nine times, the padres' patience was sorely tried and the corn supply dwindled alarmingly!

But gentile Indians were very friendly and brought gifts of pine nuts and seeds which they made into porridge as the scanty food supply lowered in bins.

Then in October, just four short months later, when all was going well and every day counted against the time when winter rains would start, Captain Fages came back and took away the three mariners, the corporal, and the young soldiers whose hands and strong backs had been so helpful to the newly founded encampment of God.

It was necessary, Captain Fages said. The lagoons at the

mouth of the Salinas had been supplying mission troops at Monterey with salt and the extra was being sent to San Blas on the king's ships. Salt was a royal monopoly and it was necessary to have a guard over it. This guard had been ordered by the government. Indians had been brought from the mission near Monterey to gather all the salt from the three lagoons into one pile and fire it with brush so a hard crust would stop the melting. Later more Indians packed it in leather bags brought from San Blas for the purpose. The salt was stored in Monterey in charge of the paymaster until it could be shipped. All this took guards to watch, for men had been found stealing, even those who transported it.

There was a sad leave-taking as soldiers gazed longingly toward those buildings created out of their own dreams and labor, standing unfinished and naked in the hot sun. Young Soberanes was among those Captain Fages took, and he wanted the worst way to stay. The soldier felt that Fages was merely showing authority because he was jealous of the interest and ambition of soldiers in the mission. There was constant trouble between the venerable Serra and Fages.

All building now had to be stopped. Only lazy older soldiers who knew they didn't have to work were left, and the two or three new ones Fages had brought took a leaf out of books of lazy ones, and would not turn a hand to help. There were now only two padres to be carpenters, blacksmiths, overseers, and farmers, with two converted Indians brought from Lower California to help them; and so many mouths to feed. The padres prayed that new Indians who came to the mission would not pattern after the gambling lazy soldiers.

In the year that followed, near starvation came upon those valiant struggling ones at San Antonio. Junípero Serra was gone to Mexico City to give an accounting of his missions, and boats bringing much needed supplies didn't arrive. They were certainly lost at sea. Padres sang out courageously at each dawn their canticle of faith in the new day, and even as empty stomachs complained they still pushed on at snail's pace with construction of irrigation ditches in an effort to water the land and drive off drought.

It was then that the pagans, those savage children, showed their love for the padres. They went out into dry hills and brought back quantities of seed and acorns to be ground into meal. They snared squirrels and rabbits and antelopes to feed the encampment. They carried wood for fires, and then, seeing lazy soldiers confessing, they asked padres if that would help them with this new God.

Captain Fages, evidently plagued by a guilty conscience, returned the corporal, and as a bonus gave the mission eight pack mules with six pack saddles and two saddle mules. Seeing the suffering, he appointed some of his men to go with him to the place Portola had called Cañada de los Osos (canyon of bears). There they shot grizzlies and sent them back to the mission for meat, and thus he was able to relieve the distress caused by the terrible shortage of food.

Indians were so impressed by the soldiers killing these great grizzlies that had long made life dangerous for them that it is recorded they became converts out of gratitude and the little mission was helped indirectly as well as directly by the slaying of the bears.

With patience and courage and sweating brows as well as faith in God, the padres toiled on. The rounding up of wild cattle with only inexperienced Indians to help. The clouds of throat-choking dust. The raucous bawling. Then the green promise of spring again with a yellow blaze of mustard. The killing for tallow, and the rendering for candles to shine on the altar. The call to evening prayers when body muscles ached and made it hard for the mind to dwell on things of the spirit. Spent bodies on mats never felt the hardness. The Canticle of Dawn again. Green growing into gold, and the fear for pasture animals until the rain came to swell the hard, curled-up corners of dried mud and blot away once more the crazy patterns in creek bottoms. And then a padre's dream materialized! In 1773, two years after its founding, there were one hundred and fifty-eight converts, and two bushels of wheat were sown and irrigated by the new ditch that a padre opened for the first time.

A new adobe church was already started farther up the canyon where two streams met and a better supply of water was at hand. Wet weather had been utilized to float logs downstream. The Mission San Antonio had survived drought and starvation and wet. There was great thanksgiving on St. Anthony's day at the mission.

5

Colonists

THE OLD ADAGE that nothing succeeds like success was proving true at San Antonio. Indians came from the hills to see these new people who had settled in their valley. They tasted corn and beans and saw that here would always be food, and so were caught by yellow rows of corn and beans from seed pods larger than ever they had seen before. They joined their fellows and became converts of San Antonio. Once converted there was no legal escape for those children of nature until the royal Spanish government should give them release—the time when emancipation meant taxation in the form of annual tribute!

Padres were indeed busy, for the converts were many now and each convert brought the work of his hands and his back to field and pasture. The missionaries believed that, if an Indian's soul was to be saved and his mind awakened, his body must first be enslaved to make him worthy. Padres forbade these neophytes to associate with the soldiers or to learn Spanish lest they learn also the white man's bad habits. They worked hard nights by tallow light to learn the gentiles' language, while the converts were locked up in a compound to prevent their running away and to keep their minds untainted.

Once in a while, when an Indian grew tired of laboring for these new people and ran away to his gentile friends to be free and fish and hunt, with no bell to call him to sweat in the fields or to make adobe bricks, he was hunted down like an antelope or a rabbit by soldiers, until he could run no longer, then brought back and whipped by them. The priests were sad over these times, but believed that discipline must be administered by soldiers so that Indians would look kindly upon padres and church. Many soldiers were unnecessarily cruel, as if they would vent their spleen at being sent so far away from Mexico City and its gaiety. They lived only for the day when their period of service would be completed. Until then, there were only Indians to show authority over, and an occasional cockfight or a bit of gambling to while away the time.

In five years San Antonio was prosperous. Stock bred from the few cattle Portola had brought from Mexico flourished and the irrigation ditches built at careful gradient down the canyons worked perfectly. Indians were good and labored well, and there was no trouble along the Salinas.

There was great rejoicing in 1776 when padres welcomed De Anza and his colonists; rejoicing not because colonists had come, for padres felt that the land belonged to the Indians and was only in trust to padres until the neophytes were trained in body and soul to take care of themselves. There was rejoicing because the young soldier José Maria Soberanes was one of De Anza's party. Shyly young Soberanes told the padres that he was soon to marry a girl who had come with De Anza's colonists. She was Ana Josefa Castro. They would live at the mission on the Carmelo near Monterey, where he was stationed. He was ready to settle down now. Hadn't he been all over Alta California on expeditions first with Portola, then Fages, and now last of all, Don Bautista De Anza? A man must settle down at twenty-three and commence having a family if *ever* he was to settle down. Then someday, when he had served his country well as a soldier, Soberanes told the padres, perhaps he could come again into the valley of the Salinas and have a rancho of his own with cattle roaming through grass and yellow mustard belly high, and so many children that there would be a name-day fiestas to celebrate in every month of the year.

Never before had a soldier carried away in his heart such blessings from padres as did young Soberanes, when he left again with the De Anza party. He was a good kindly soldier who understood Indians and never punished cruelly. This young lover wanted to live in the valley of the Salinas and found a big family to the glory of God and the king of Spain!

6

A Dreamer

THE EARLY COLONISTS were a sorry lot and tried the patience of padres even more than did the Indians. While San Antonio flourished through hard work and sweat, the colonists sat waiting for supply boats to come from Mexico. It was easier to wait in the shade than to work in the sun. They were so poor that they had to be supplied with food and clothes by the government, even to ribbons for their queues. Some were disgruntled because they were to be paid in advance for coming to settle in the new country. But since they were mostly gamblers and if paid in money would have nothing, clothes and equipment were the pay including ribbons for hats and hair, and chemises and petticoats for the women. All this to keep up their morale in the wilderness.

Padres resented these lazy colonists and considered them a poor example for Indians, but they "let out" Indian labor without charge to help the new rancheros, and loaned each settler ten or twelve cattle and sheep from mission stock as a start. These were to be returned in a few years when there was enough increase.

But what was the use of working? Spain would allow no trade with this new colony. What would they do with the increase? As for meat it was far easier to approach a deer or an antelope than the wild range cattle. Only a few were ambitious enough to build habitable homes. The rest went

to church, openly yearned to be back in Old Spain or Mexico, and showed an uncommon interest in the aguardiente
the padres made from grapes, apples, and pears. They were
fascinated with the construction of the great circular bode-
gas, or wine vats, that missionaries were building in the
compound at San Antonio.

Gradually most of the colonists drifted toward Monterey and ships that would take them back to the fleshpots.

At San Antonio the business of soul-saving thrived
beyond the wildest expectation of the padres. There was
now a population of 1,076 neophytes and San Antonio was
the largest mission community in California just as the venerable Juníper Serra, now long dead, had predicted when he
rang the bells from an oak tree nineteen years before. Cattle
and flocks had multiplied; corn and beans were plentiful
because now a ditch had been extended to water many thousand acres of bottom land. The Indians labored well and
gave little trouble.

There were so many converts that a new mission was
needed on the wide plain of the Salinas. Perhaps this decision
for extending the good work was helped by the convenient
resignation of Governor Fages, who from the very first expedition as captain had opposed the wishes of the padres and
made their work harder than it needed to be. They felt less
oppressed under the new governor.

On October 9, 1791, the padres took Indians, stock,
seeds, and implements and walked over the mountains and
down onto the wide plain of the Salinas. They raised the
cross on the spot where Portola and his disgruntled soldiers
had camped under willows beside the river, and they called
the new mission Nuestra Señora de la Soledad (Our Lady of
Solitude), because wind whistled so mournfully, like a saint
crying in the wilderness for the sorrows of sinning men.

A great cry of joy went up when the padres from San

W.K.Fisher

THE MISSION O

AN ANTONIO DE PADUA

Antonio saw that José Maria Soberanes, now a seasoned soldier of thirty-eight, was to be stationed at the new mission. Soberanes' dream of a big family and a rancho in the Salinas still persisted. He already had considerable family with the promise of more to come and he was again stationed in the Salinas. There remained only the realization of stock on his own land grazing up to their bellies in grass.

Wind moaned around the little mud-and-tule Mission of Our Lady of Solitude and converts were slow in coming to God, so slow that at the end of the first year there was only a baker's dozen. The padre sweated on, planning and building irrigation ditches against dry years. Soberanes the soldier dreamed on about the future, dreams of smiling plenty for himself and his sons and his sons' sons, on a rancho in the Valley of the Salinas.

PART II

Soldiers

Land

SOBERANES had not dreamed in vain. In 1795 six provisional land grants were made by the governor in Alta California. Buena Vista, a rancho of 8,446.23 acres in the Valley of the Salinas went to José Maria Soberanes and his father-in-law, Joaquin Castro. At forty-two Soberanes was pensioned off to become a ranchero. Before the year was out one hundred and fifty head of cattle roamed the land up to their bellies in feed, and Indian labor had completed the low adobe house that was to mark the Soberanes beginnings in the valley of winds. But success had its price for man and for mission.

Malcontents among returned colonists had evidently told in Mexico and in Spain about the padres at San Antonio living in plenty; told of the wine vats and orchards, and about the hot springs that were a part of Soledad's vineyard, where padres bathed and relaxed weary bodies in warm soothing waters of the paradise they called Paraíso Springs. All this stirred up the politicians.

Supply ships brought less and less to do with, as if those in power would starve out the missions by denying materials which they could not raise on the land. Now and then a forbidden trader put into the Bay of Monterey and there was exchange of many mission hides and sea otter skins for a few of the necessities of life. The provincial governor

somehow learned of this smuggling, for he sent a stiff procla-
mation saying that priests must have no dealing with foreign
vessels. The padre replied promptly from Mission Soledad
that it would give him pleasure to comply with the order if
ever Divine Providence should favor this mission, forty
miles inland, with a harbor. Then he continued his treks to
Monterey with hides to be smuggled out for the necessary
supplies. Was he, the guardian of these people, to see the
mission waste away in its struggle with the soil, because
despots in Spain decreed there was to be no trade with the
colony? Surely the good St. Francis would forgive him a
little smuggling for bare necessities to carry on.

But politicians were now hot on the trail of the padres.
An expedition was sent to see why the colony was not being
settled except by a handful of retired soldiers and their
families. Was this sparse settlement because padres wanted
to hold the land for their own interests? Word had come
that the missionaries discouraged settlers.

Malaspina, the officer in charge of the expedition, was
impressed with this new Alta California and evidently
shocked to learn of the shameful way Spain had neglected
the colony. He discovered that there were no boats and that
trade was forbidden. Among other things he found out that
José Maria Soberanes had dressed ninety-five sea otter skins
for the government and received $55 for the work. The
government of Spain was carrying on a monopoly with
China, to trade sea otter pelts for quicksilver. These skins
from the coast near Monterey went to line the robes of
mandarins in China and Spain received the quicksilver. What
was California receiving? She was drained of her resources
and left to fight her own battles in the wilderness. Trade
with the outside was forbidden. How could this system
bring colonists to develop the land?

When Malaspina returned to Spain he was frank in
his criticism of the government's misrule of her New World

possessions. This led to his arrest and imprisonment for eight years and finally banishment from Spain. His carefully prepared reports never saw print!

Work must go on at the missions in the Salinas to feed and care for Indians in spite of government expeditions. The padres at Soledad had their hands full with cattle roundup and branding, for now missions had to brand their cattle to identify them from the animals of colonists and stock that belonged to the "King's Pasture," which was used to supply the soldiers at the Presidio over in Monterey. Mis-

MISSION CATTLE BRANDS

San Antonio · Padre Doroteo Ambris · San Miguel
(SAN ANTONIO)

sion Soledad was very close to the King's Pasture, where disgruntled, poorly paid soldiers rounded up cattle; care must be taken to protect mission stock from the too eager soldiery.

The politicians hadn't forgotten. Missions were too prosperous for the comfort of some in Mexico City and in Spain. Another expedition was sent to investigate conditions, this time led by Captain Costansa, the engineer and mapmaker who had come with Portola. Why were there only thirty families in all Alta California, in spite of the government help these settlers were given?

Costansa reported to his superiors that the mission plan for colonization was a failure, and after so many years the mission lands still remained in the hands of padres. This alone accounted for the lack of people. The padres felt obligated to care for Indians and claimed that the land belonged to their converts. Padres discouraged settlement because they didn't want Indians to be influenced by habits and sins learned from Spaniards and Mexicans. Padres wanted to *control* the colony.

Costansa felt that the land grants did not belong to the church or to mission establishments but to the crown. Indians, of course, were recognized owners under the crown of what land they needed for their support and that was all. He recommended to his government that missions were to function for only ten years and then should be turned into settlements and the missionaries returned to their convents.

Those hard-working padres were not to be turned from their course so easily. They reminded all concerned in Mexico and Spain of the old law that came from Spain: the Law of the Indios, now an international law, which held that an Indian was a minor for life and as such could not own property. This law had been made in 1492 when Pope Alexander VI first drew the line of demarcation. Thus it was necessary to have guardians over Indian property to see that no harm came to those who espoused the church. The padres were doing this and without them the Indians would be lost.

And so it was that a Spanish pope three hundred years before brought troubles to the Salinas. Those in high places in Spain were too wise to go directly against the church, but missions were too prosperous; they now had thousands of cattle, the increase from animals the government had sent. Padres must pay taxes. They must pay with hides and tallow for the privilege of running missions and converting Indians to the Faith.

Mission taxes were paid. Padres and Indians worked

harder than ever to raise enough hides and tallow to satisfy Spain's demands. The differences between the struggling missionaries and the government now seemed to become a matching of wits. Fearing that the ten-year plan for missions might go into effect in spite of the Law of the Indios, the padres took means to ensure the future of their childlike converts. They raised the cross in still another part of the great Valley of the Salinas. This time farther south.

Our Lady of Solitude and San Antonio contributed cattle, horses, and sheep to start the new mission named San Miguel (St. Michael). The padre from San Antonio, now fifty-eight but still full of courage and zeal, was directed by the presidente of missions to lay the foundation and stay at the new mission until it was well-started. Fifteen children were baptized on the founding day. Now, if the ten-year plan went into effect and San Antonio was turned into a settlement and Indians left to their own devices, and Our Lady of Solitude had to follow, there would still be padres to watch over God's flocks in the valley of the winds.

But taxes on missions were high. So *many* hides, so *many* bladders of tallow each year went out. Missions were drained. Padres in the church at Monterey remembered that the Buena Vista grant made to Soberanes the soldier was only a *provisional* grant of land that belonged to them. The governor had promised that when the mission needed this land it would be restored. The mission needed it now to raise more cattle so that taxes could be met. They demanded the land. Soberanes must go.

José Maria Soberanes the pensioner was heartsick. For seven years he had worked and struggled on the land. His alone of all the grants along the Salinas had survived. Two had been destroyed by savage Indians, the others abandoned. The Mission San Carlos *couldn't* take his land and his dream home away from him now. He had a big family to look out for—sons and daughters to carry on and be good Catholic citizens in this new country. He appealed to the governor himself for justice. The governor refused to evict Soberanes, but death, no respecter of padres or governor, took the ambitious Spanish soldier out of the Salinas the year after the governor himself declared no one could force him off. Soberanes' widow moved to Monterey with her family. Her son Feliciano, now sixteen, would follow his father and be a soldier in the Presidio there.

Buena Vista Rancho again became a wilderness of yellow mustard. Wind blew through window and door openings of the low adobe; swallows and bats took possession of José Maria's house of dreams. On clear moonlight nights coyotes screamed across the plain from near-by foothills. The soldier's beloved land once more belonged to the crown of Spain.

2

Taxes and Troubles

T HE NEW Mission of San Miguel had nearly a thousand converts now and a herd coming on. San Antonio was
going its way by hard work. Our Lady of Solitude had five
hundred converts, and over a thousand head of cattle and
several thousand sheep cropped the hillsides with Indian
herders to watch them. A great irrigation system was built
at Soledad by Indian labor to wrest subsistence from twenty
thousand acres of parched earth in the Salinas Valley.

But in spite of all this toiling there was short shrift
for the missions in the valley of winds. Indians must be fed,
and padres buried more than they baptized these days, for
epidemics as well as taxes had spread over the land. Soldiers
had not been paid and were resentful of Indian converts
they guarded at missions; they pilfered from mission store-
houses. Perhaps this lack of pay was part of the diabolical
plan to help breed trouble and bring on a revolt against the
missions.

The good-natured, snuff-taking priest at Soledad did
his best to quiet the trouble with soldiers by treating them
well and teaching them to read and write to help them get
advancement. It may have been a matter of politics rather
than kind heart, for soldiers at his mission knew about the
forbidden smuggling of hides to ships in Monterey.

Now the colony was used as a dumping ground for

criminals, drunks, and foundlings from the streets of Mexico City. They were sent to California as punishment and were a lazy, good-for-nothing lot. Even Botany Bay criminals had been left on the shore at the point of a gun near Monterey, and crazed with scurvy and half-starved they had made their way to the missions. Decent colonists of the sparsely settled district resented all these undesirables but there was nothing to do. They had their own troubles with imported cattle thieves and troublemakers. Alta California was the land Spain taxed and forgot. The mother country kept her boats away so that many people could not attend church for want of clothes!

In 1816 church attendance fell off so sharply that a law was passed: "All persons must attend mass and respond in a loud voice. If they fail to do so they will be put in stocks four hours."

Many a fine New England mansion was built and handsomely furnished on furs and hides and tallow smuggled out of the Salinas Valley to a "Boston" ship in the port of Monterey by half-starved padres. On one voyage a Boston ship purchased 560 sea otter skins worth six thousand dollars, in half a day, with goods worth a dollar and a half in Boston. But then California wasn't Boston! The same skins sold for twenty-three dollars each in Canton, but California wasn't Canton! Another sailing vessel captain received eight thousand dollars' worth of furs for a rusty chisel.

Russians came down from the north and brought expert Aleut hunters and in one year took away eighty thousand sea otter skins, without anyone to stop them. Padres sent urgent appeals about this to the governor, for he was a kind governor, but he seemed helpless, and Spain was too far away to care what went on in Alta California.

Some politicians in high places claimed the padres had great wealth of cattle and land and were misrepresenting this value when they made reports.

Not until 1818, when Bouchard, the Argentinian pirate, and his Sandwich Islanders came into the Bay of Monterey to burn and pillage, did even the unpaid soldiers take an interest in what went on! That affected their homes and their families. People of Monterey and Santa Cruz fled to the King's Pasture in the Valley of the Salinas, and to the Mission Soledad, for sanctuary. Soldiers with a few colonists and untrained Indians made a feeble effort to resist the plundering pirates, and then promptly retreated.

José Mariano Estrada, a mission soldier, was one of these unpaid disgruntled leaders sent out to fight pirates. He had come soldiering to the new country in 1797 and was now a man with grown sons and daughters. As he sat on the hillside with his comrades in arms, and helplessly watched the destruction of Monterey, he began talking to Feliciano Soberanes, son of José Maria and a member of the militia at the Presidio. Feliciano was married, with four children now and another on the way, a child for every year of his marriage to Antonia Rodriquez.

What was the future for soldiers? they asked each other. How long were they to stay in the wilderness with families to raise and no pay? The missions were doomed. Feliciano was only thirty-one; soldiering was all he knew, but he thought land was the answer. Already he had petitioned for the fine Rancho Sausal (willow grove) in the Salinas, not too far from the mouth, where sea fogs made the climate good. He was going there with his family as soon as the governor granted him the land. One day he would be a don with thousands of cattle roaming the land, and Indians to labor, and nothing to do but ride and rest and enjoy himself. He and his brother Mariano were going to apply for even more land.

Estrada saw the good in that. Land *was* the answer. He had sons grown now who could claim grants. There was the place the wife of old José Maria Soberanes had abandoned, the Buena Vista, with over seven thousand acres of good land. That would do as a starter. Then his sons Santiago and Pedro could take the next abandoned rancho to Buena Vista, the Llano de Buena Vista, and that had over eight thousand acres. Fifteen thousand acres and more would be better than waiting around a mission for lieutenant's pay that never came. They would have a rancho worth the name, would the Estradas. He, too, would have a fine horse and a fine saddle and be a landed don. There was a plan fomenting to free Mexico from Spain, to secede; and once freed, trade would come and California would thrive. Land was the answer. He, Estrada, would petition soon. The governor would never refuse a request from a soldier. The Valley of the Salinas had once more charmed the king's soldiers to leave barracks for the land.

3

Freedom—1822

T HE CHANGE came rapidly, even before José Estrada had a chance to apply to the Spanish governor for land in the Salinas. Mexico had revolted against the despotism of Spain. A half-Indian, Agustin de Iturbide, had led the revolt and become the Liberator of Mexico! He called himself Emperor Iturbide. But there was trouble about Iturbide. Mexico wanted to be a republic, with no emperors, no kings!

How did the struggling ones in the Valley of the Salinas know all this? Riders came over the Santa Lucias, eyes fired with excitement and horses a-lather to tell that a ship flying a flag of green, white, and red, with an eagle and a crown in the center, had put into Monterey harbor. A boat manned by oarsmen put off from the ship and landed their leader on shore. This leader had presented himself to the comandante and told that he had come from the imperial Mexican capital with word directed to the governor of this province. He demanded the governor in the name of his sovereign, the Liberator of Mexico, General Don Agustin de Iturbide.

There was great rejoicing along the Salinas. Carefully hoarded powder was shot off in celebration and aguardiente flowed. California was free from Spain at last. Mexico would start trade. Ships from all over the world would come to Monterey for Salinas Valley hides and tallow.

The padre at Soledad was solemn; he refused to swear

allegiance to any foreign power, for word had come to him by underground that Mexicans had seized the great Pious Fund that had been raised long ago for missions. Without that fund the missions could not exist even in their present half-starved state.

The padre was threatened with arrest for refusing to celebrate mass in honor of "freedom." He was so beloved and so powerful among Indians that officers were afraid to banish him or to do away with him for fear of stirring up a hornet's nest. Already there had been enough trouble with Indians in revolt. The man of God merely remained under arrest on the plain of the Salinas, where wind howled mournfully around Our Lady of Solitude, and a thousand Indians each day sang the Canticle to the Dawn and then went to work in the five hundred square miles of irrigated fields.

Iturbide abdicated soon and was shot for leading Indians against the government. Mexico was a republic, and the Pious Fund was gone forever.

José Estrada was granted Buena Vista by the first Mexican governor for his part in heading the local skirmishes, and his sons were granted Llano Buena Vista. All the Estradas and their families went to live in the Salinas.

Feliciano, son of José Maria Soberanes, had land now, too, and five children with another on the way. Rancho Sausal was his, and he and his brother already had their eyes on another fine place of 5,941 acres, the Rancho Alisal (alder grove). Landed dons were in the making along the Salinas.

PART III

Three Traders and Their Wedding Rings

I

A Lancashire Lad Arrives

WHEN THE MEXICANS took over Alta California from Spain in 1822 there were only thirteen foreigners in the whole of the land: three Americans, two Scotchmen, two Englishmen, one Irishman, one Russian, one Portuguese, and three Negroes from the West Indies.

But now California was free. Mexico wanted it settled. Lands would be granted to all who could make use of them: Mexican citizens without distinction, except special consideration due to private merit and service to the country. Comandantes of presidios could make grants, and alcaldes of settlements could grant pueblo lots; larger grants were made by the governor. A league, or 4,438.56 acres, was a unit and eleven of these, or 48,824.16 acres, could be granted to one person. This would colonize the wilderness.

Word went around the world calling all men to come and claim their golden bounty from this new land. Adventurous ones who were to make the laws and bring prosperity to the Salinas were soon on their way in sailing ships.

Among the first traders to arrive was William E. P. Hartnell, a young Lancashire man. He came to purchase hides and tallow for a shopkeeper of Lima, Peru.

Hartnell had charm and wit and an education and knew how to use all three to the best advantage. He lost no time around the port of Monterey where "Boston" ships were now openly carrying on their trade in sea otter skins that would be exchanged in China for silks to dress New England women, and tea to be gossiped over of cold afternoons on Beacon Street. He bought horses and rode into the Valley of the Salinas to size up what this new country was like, away from the old Spanish capital of Monterey.

Missions had cattle and padres were sorely in need of trade. That, the blond Anglo-Saxon decided, was the way to begin.

At Mission San Miguel the padre stopped work on the new adobe church that was to replace the temporary one, and he listened to this trader. After wine and a few tortillas and beans, the padre sold Hartnell a contract on all the hides, tallow, and other mission products for three years. The company Hartnell represented was bound to send one vessel a year to take all hides offered and at least 312 tons of tallow, and to pay in money and goods!

They looked off over the golden plain where Indians labored and cattle grazed. There was more wine to celebrate this good bargain. A merchant had come to the Salinas. The first mercantile business on the Pacific coast had its beginnings that day in the Mission San Miguel. The Valley of the Salinas was to claim a trader different from smugglers, a trader, more scholar than businessman, one educated in English and German universities, who dreamed of fine things to come and then went about bringing his dreams into three dimensions.

Hartnell was eager to live in this new land of opportunity. He liked the climate and the companionship of the learned padres, for those hard-working friars were realists and philosophers as well as soul-savers. Perhaps best of all, young William liked the dark-eyed señoritas.

But he, William E. P. Hartnell, was an outsider, a Protestant, and the country was Catholic. In order to love or to own land one must first be a Catholic. He set up his mer-

cantile business in Monterey, then began to study his catechism. There was no time to be lost!

To Hartnell this was a strange land of contradictions,
of frontier and of caste such as he had never seen before.

W. E. P. HARTNELL

It was a country where men of the church in worn home-
spun robes worked in the fields alongside of Indian laborers
in the very struggle for existence to pay high taxes imposed
on missionary establishments; a country where one drop of
Spanish blood entitled the bearer to the best there was, and
a bullock driver spoke soft Castilian Spanish after the man-

ner of a diplomat. No one worked but padres and Indians.

Many men could neither read nor write, but they spent long hours perfecting their rubrics—those flourishes that went around and under their names to prevent forgery and make the signature legal. These fancy loops and curlicues were used by Californians instead of a seal. The higher the social standing, the more ornate the rubric. Some signatures covered half a foolscap page.

In the old Spanish capital women wore velvet cloaks and trod the bare earth floors of their windowless adobes in spangled satin slippers. Hides served over openings for doors, but each house had many Indian servants, and gowns were imported from France. Men used the legs of a horse to go even a few yards, and it was the wife's daily duty to comb and braid the long hair of her husband.

The Customs House in Monterey now did a good business, for traders were required to list their stocks and pay taxes when they put into port. There was only a shrug of shoulders when some collectors' wives had shawls and new silk dresses, and some traders paid little or no taxes.

Trade in hides and tallow went on all along the coast. Hartnell sold his goods and took the promise of hides and tallow to be delivered the next year or eighteen months. Sometimes a ranchero sent a hair from his head as a guarantee to pay and his wife had a tasty new calico to wear a year before it was paid for.

It is not on record whether great ambition or the gentle eyes of a pious young señorita spurred young Hartnell on toward baptism. He had met the lovely little Teresa de la Guerra, when he went over the grade from the Salinas to Santa Barbara for trade with the mission there. She was a gay young spinster in her early teens and knew how to use her eyes to charm this new man who fascinated all the girls with his winning ways and skin light-colored as milk. She liked to dance. Within a year the young William was baptized at Mission San Carlos in Monterey. Now W. E. P. Hartnell, the Lancashire lad, was a Mexican citizen with the right to claim as many as 48,824 acres of land; and, if he was lucky, to claim as his bride a young Californian from one of the high-caste Spanish families in Santa Barbara. Things were looking up.

A Scotch Salter and a Peruvian

THE WASTE at slaughtertime was enough to sicken an Englishman. After the hides and tallow was taken, thousands of carcasses were left on the wide plain of the Salinas to rot in the sun. Great bands of dogs were kept at each mission for scavenger purposes, but the remainder was left for California condors, buzzards, coyotes, and bluebottles. Maybe Hartnell thought of people in London slums who rarely had a chance to eat a bit of meat, and the waste hurt him, or perhaps he was merely interested in trade, in getting ahead. Whatever the motive, he was not long in managing a contract to cheat the buzzards and supply the Peruvian government with salt meat as a side line to the hides and tallow business. Expert salters must be imported to prepare the meat for shipment.

And so it was that in 1824 young David Spence, a blue-eyed Scot from Huntley came sailing into Monterey Bay. He brought a number of salters and coopers from Ireland and Scotland, who were to prepare the meat under his supervision and barrel it for shipment to Peru.

For some reason the meat branch of the business was unprofitable, and after a few cargoes had been shipped, it was abandoned. There was no market for meat. Only the best cuts were saved for household use and the rest left to raise a stench.

This free country of great spaces appealed to young David. In Scotland no poor person could ever own land. The peers had it all, and you rented it until you were planted in the graveyard, with always hanging over you the worry of rent and what "the laird of the manor" wanted you to do. Here a chap could own land for himself as far as eye could see, just by being a Catholic and claiming Mexican citizenship, without two coins in his pocket to jingle one against the other. Besides, the dark-eyed lassies here fancied a blue-eyed Scotchman as a bit of a change, and that warmed the cockles of the heart, if ever anything could, especially when a title to land often went along with the lassie to her marriage bed. He was staying on in the new country, salt meat or none. They had their classes here as well as in Scotland, but any chap who had plenty of land could be a "don," although he be born across the sea on a moor purple with heather. Don David Spence he would be, riding over his land on a fine horse with a silver-trimmed bridle. His children would never know what it was not to own land of their own.

The young Scot worked on with Hartnell, studied his catechism betweentimes, and decided that little Adelaida Estrada was as likely a lassie as ever California had produced. Her father, Don Mariano Estrada, was comandante of Monterey and he had Rancho Buena Vista, some of the best land in the Valley of the Salinas. Adelaida's sister was married to the rich Peruvian trader, Juan Malarin, who already had fifty thousand acres of land farther north. David Spence knew about these Peruvian Malarins; they were toffs, grandees. Juan Malarin had been chosen by the government to take the prizes *Asia* and *Constante* to Acapulco, and for this service he had been made a lieutenant in the Mexican Navy. He was a quiet unobtrusive man with a fine character and lots of influence in these parts. It would be well for a Scotchman to be related to Juan Malarin by marriage; he would then be among the best.

The Scot was baptized David Esteban Spence at the mission in Santa Cruz in 1828 and then, catechism learned, he was able to spend his spare time courting Adelaida Estrada. He was encouraged, because not long before John Cooper the trader had been baptized Juan Bautista Cooper and had married Encarnacion Vallejo, a girl of thirteen and sister to one of Mexico's higher-ups in this new land. There was still talk about the grand wedding in Santa Barbara when William Hartnell claimed little Teresa de la Guerra.

There had been days of celebration at Santa Barbara, and then a wedding procession all the way from Santa Barbara to Monterey. A trail had to be cut through mustard fifteen feet high, for Hartnell and his bride, and couriers rode first to make arrangements at scattered ranchos in the Salinas for the bridal couple to stay each nightfall. There was a fiesta at every rancho, with fine things to eat, and wine brought miles by oxcart from vineyards to the north. Everybody in the district came and there was dancing until cockcrow. When a California bride was Spanish, wine flowed freely in the land, and she found open house wherever she went.

Such a pother as weddings were in this new land, it made young Spence fair weary just to contemplate the idea. There was no popping into a parsonage and having a parson say the words and have done with it. There were the banns to be read three Sundays in church, for all to know the intentions of both parties. Meanwhile a man had to pick out six of everything the bride wore as his gift to her: six dresses, six rebozos, six mantillas, six beaded jackets, six pairs of satin shoes (and if he was very sentimental the bridegroom made the white satin shoes for her wedding with his own hands). Then there were the ribbons and earrings and pearls brought from La Paz where the divers seemed to know when a man was needing bridal finery and put up the price. The dresses must be fine ones from Paris or England and cost around a hundred dollars. But it was worth it all if you let the head as well as the heart plan for the future.

But David Spence sighed over it all. There was the wedding morning when the lassie went to church all dressed in black to confess her sins before she married and a man could scarce keep his own mind on his "Father, bless me" for wondering what manner of sins his wife-to-be was confessing.

Then the procession to the church when she had changed her dress and came forth in shining white to ride on the horse in front of her godfather or in a carreta trimmed in flowers, while Indians and paisanos lined the road to look for the last time at her dainty ankles and old women held their black shawls close and cried and blew their noses, because she would soon no longer be a carefree girl, but initiated into the mysteries of marriage.

There was the ceremony in Latin and Spanish and then the bridesmaid stooping to take the pins from the bride's long dress, so that from this moment on no man but her husband should see her ankles!

The wedding fiesta and the toasts, "a su provecho" (may you prosper) over and over, and the matron of honor waiting outside the nuptial chamber for a report from the bridegroom that his bride was a virgin and all was well, or to learn that things were not well and she would need to wear her hair cut off for all to know that she had been tasting the joys of love before a wedding ring had been placed on her finger. Days of feasting and foolery, when sometimes a man's wife was kidnapped by pranksters and he had to pay a ransom of wine to get her back. All this he, David Esteban Spence, must go through before he could make Adelaida Estrada his own.

It was well-known that these hijas del país (daughters of the country) found it easy to fall in love with blue-eyed men, and that Spaniards were very jealous. A Scot must be canny and forget the ways of the Scottish heath, and do things the way the Mexicans did them. In 1829 they were married.

PART IV

Hides and Tallow, Happiness and Ease

I

Drought

Padres at San Miguel rising from their knees after prayers looked up at the beautiful decoration on the wall of their new church. While his house was being built in Monterey young Esteban Munras, the grantee of Rancho San Vicente, had spent a year at the mission with his bride, painting the "All-Seeing Eye" and the delicately tinted conch shells as his tribute to the Blessed Sacrament. But now the "All-Seeing Eye" of God looked down on worried padres.

All was not well with missions along the Salinas. So many changes in politics. Petty revolutions were frequently brought on by men in desperate circumstances at the bottom of the ladder who wanted to climb and used the missions as tools. Hides and tallow must be given first to one tax collector, and then before many moons another officer of the Mexican government came to claim still another payment. There was no more aid from the Pious Fund. Some traders let greed enter into the yearly bargain over mission stock and took more than the fifty-fifty agreed upon. Padres couldn't be everywhere to watch during matanza time, when in a single day there were sometimes two thousand cattle slaughtered for their hides and tallow. These matanzas, or slaughters, were the climax of the year's toil, worry, and sweat, when bands of men on horseback rode fast through the pastures with knives. They passed an animal, gave it a blow in the neck with a knife, and it fell dead. These brave ones were the nuqueadores (neckers) and were followed by many skinners who took off the hides. Next came butchers who cut the best meat into strips for drying. Last of all trudged mission Indian women to gather tallow in leather bags or blad-

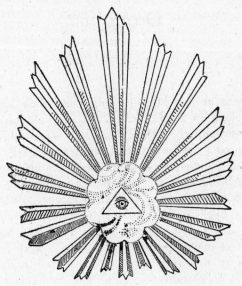

ESTEBAN MUNRAS' ALL-SEEING
EYE—SAN MIGUEL MISSION

ders. Offal was left for the hundreds of dogs kept at each mission for the purpose.

The matanza at San Miguel was over for another year. While the padres figured long and closely by the light of tallow candles to see how the mission would fare, grizzlies and coyotes made fiesta among the carcasses on the lonely plain; and soldiers, disgruntled at seeing so many hides, grumbled about lack of pay. Indians sensing trouble were restless and dissatisfied with meager mission fare.

After L·A·FUERTES 03

CALIFORNIA VULTURE
Beneficiary of Matanzas

For settlers along the Salinas, hides and tallow meant a different story. Cattle "borrowed" from mission stock and Indian labor, "let out" free of charge by the padres, brought them happiness and ease.

From dawn until after dusk these rancheros could not exist without hides and tallow. In the morning they pulled on calfskin clothes and shoes, and sat on chair seats made of hide with the hair still on it to eat meat and cheese with horn knives and forks. They washed dishes with soap that Indians made from tallow mixed with ashes and carried along jerked beef when they rode in leather saddles to rope cattle with rawhide riatas. Oxen pulled wooden wheeled carts that were lashed together with thongs. Women used tallow mixed with rose petals as perfume and cream for the skin and to brighten the hair. Tallow candles lighted adobes when night came and hides were dropped over doors and windows to keep out the cold air. Sometimes the very walls of adobes were reinforced by a row of skulls with the horns still on them.

Children were conceived and born and men died in beds made from hides stretched over a wooden frame.

These great stiff "California banknotes" paid their taxes and kept the families of many rancheros in luxury at the gay capital of Monterey.

All this, because long ago zealous padres brought two hundred cattle on the long trek from New Spain to this wilderness province of California.

New Yankee traders were fattening off the hides and botas of tallow and the extravagant ideas of the wilderness dwellers. Ships went out with as many as thirty thousand hides, for which they had exchanged manufactured goods, including shoes made in Massachusetts from Salinas Valley hides. These shoes were bought at prices many times what they would have brought in Boston. Hides were worth two dollars each and twenty-five pounds of tallow went for a dollar and a quarter. Shoes were sixteen to twenty dollars a pair and silk stockings and shawls sold high.

Then came the drought. Month after month padres and settlers alike searched the skies for even a cloud the size of a man's hand as indication that the good God had heard their prayers. Twelve months went by; the ground was baked hard. Pasture was more scant with each setting sun, and dumb creatures looked with lackluster eyes at the mirage of heat that deceived the senses into thinking there was a lake. Eighteen months passed. The good God was forgetting animals and men in the Salinas. Sparse settlers traveling from ranchos to the missions by horseback to confess their sins of a Saturday and stay overnight so they could take communion saw leaves of oaks and willows curling in the hot sun. Great black buzzards circled high against the clear blue sky and waited for some poor walking skeleton covered with red hide to become a carcass.

Each cool dawn the padres turned to the east and bravely sang out their canticle to the new day. Extra prayers were made at Matins, then Indians went to dig deeper the few water holes in caked creek beds in an effort to save enough animals for food. Irrigation ditches shone bleached and white in the sun, with lizards warming their bellies in the bottom, and brown ghosts of bean plants rattled their leaves in the wind, where once there had been green fields of plenty. Water holes were dried up where rancheros usually had their washing-get-togethers three times a year to feast while Indians from each rancho washed the clothes. There was scarcely water enough to have a house blessed by the padre, when the man of God went from room to room sprinkling holy water on walls and saying prayers, after which there was a good dinner and dance.

A second Judas day came, when green should be pricking through and yellow mustard and blue lupines coloring the footsteps of spring; but still no rain. This time, there was little incentive for fiesta at the missions, because Judas the traitor could not be burned in effigy, for fear fire would spread by wind into the tinder-dry hills.

Worried worshipers saw dark covering drop from the altar on Easter and the cross shine out, and they smiled at the two little angels with real white feather wings on each side of the altar, for one angel had a black eye from fighting for the privilege of being an angel. When Mass was over they went outside into the searing heat that had taken forty thousand cattle.

Young people went on flirting and being young and babies kept on being born, in holy matrimony or as little "catch colts" that came from marriage under the stars by "Father Buckeye." Old people were taken by death out of the inferno that was Salinas Valley; and still no rain.

2

The Law

SINCE THE actions of men the world over are guided
by their need for food and comfort, drought brought law-
lessness to the Salinas in 1829. Marauders roamed the country at night to steal cattle, and because many horses had been
killed in order to conserve pasture for cattle, horses were
scarce; men often took horses that didn't belong to them to
replace faithful animals that had perished. Gambling increased and liquor made trouble. There was an increase of
"catch colts." Some rancheros, finding that their prayers for
rain were not answered, ceased attending church and those
who did go on the long trek to missions were often held up
on the Soledad road by Domingo Hernandez, the robber,
who carried a string of human ears on his saddle. Hernandez
was a great robber and a keen collector. He fancied large
well-formed ears for his string and no time or place was
inopportune for the carrying on of his hobby. Pious people
coming home from church were terror-stricken just at the
sight of him. Something had to be done about this state of
affairs.

Officials at the capital in Monterey made the following
laws:

"Church duties must be strictly performed, nor must
anyone leave church when the sermon begins, as is cus-
tomary.

"Liquor is not to be sold on feast days before Mass, nor after drum-beat at night. Fine 4 to 8 dollars and confiscation of liquor.

"Every game of hazard prohibited. Penalty imprisonment at hard work or fine 5 to 10 dollars for having a game in one's house.

"No person to be out of his house after hour of la queda (bedtime) except for urgent necessity. Penalty 8 days of arrest.

"Fine of six dollars for taking a horse without the owner's consent.

"Debts for liquor and gambling cannot be collected.

"Indian servants must be called home at bedtime and employers will be responsible for their doings.

"Entering taverns or houses on horseback *strictly* prohibited. Fine 1 to 2 or 3 dollars.

"Any person who will not work will be considered a vagrant and employed in public works.

"No person shall take any article in pawn since it is a way of robbing in usury.

"These regulations apply to all persons not engaged in actual military service."

The soldier Feliciano Soberanes and his brother now lived on their second grant of nearly six thousand acres, the Alisal. The adobe house built by Indian labor was on a knoll sheltered by hills, and Soberanes could stand in his dooryard and see leafless alders and sycamores and what was left of his cattle dotting the hills and plain. Don Feliciano had eight children and another coming any minute (thanks to God). The governor had appointed him justice of peace for Alisal District and Salinas Plain and he was bound to enforce the laws on scattered rancheros in the valley.

When 1830 came and still no rain, another law was sent for Don Feliciano to enforce. The drought had made people go into debt to traders and there was already feeling about so many foreigners coming into California. "No grant of land can be taken in payment of debts of the grantee."

Old ones who had struggled wagged grizzled heads and sucked at empty tooth sockets. "Who but Satan himself would *want* land in the Salinas dry now for twenty-two months?"

And then one night rain came. A drop or two at first, stealing soft and light as any thief feeling his way in unaccustomed country. Crickets in close-cropped stubble stopped chirping, and tree toads croaked out for the first time in many moons. Noiselessly in the velvet dark caked mud swelled in creek bottoms and dried colorless lichens on the north side of bare trees softened into gray-green beauty. At dawn the padres lifted their voices in glad thanksgiving.

Rain! Rain! Children, wild with joy over the fresh morning world, ran bareheaded into the wet and opened mouths to catch drops. Cattle moved once more with spirit and all the earth was fragrant with dampness. Pious ones reminded each other of their faith that the good God would not forget them and less pious ones celebrated with long-hoarded wine. All rancheros planned once more for the future. The terrible drought was broken and that night so were the laws broken along the Salinas. Gay young caballeros rode miles to stand in the rain and serenade:

> Do not kill me with a pistol or a knife!
> Kill me rather with thine eyes, love.
> With those red lips take my life;
> Do not kill me with a pistol or a knife!

Or perhaps they sang another old favorite while they waited for the lady's candle to flicker and indicate that she had heard:

> Fly not yet, 'tis just the hour
> When pleasure like the midnight flower,

That scorns the eye of vulgar light
Begins to bloom for sons of night
And maids who love the moon.

Horses, taking the lovers home, plunged into muddy
water to their knees. The Salinas was up!

3

Fiesta and the Deepening Shadows

Drought was soon buried and forgotten in the lush growth of seasons that followed. Pious ones felt that the good earth of the Salinas was feeling remorse and giving forth extra in return for that two-year test of faith. Cattle multiplied wonderously, babies were born, the free generous life went on.

Grantees of Salinas Valley land who lived in the capital came for summers to their ranchos. Valley rancheros went visiting, complete with servants, sometimes to stay for a month at other ranchos so that often there were forty guests at once. Indian tortilla makers were kept busy from dawn to dark and a bullock slaughtered in the morning was scarce enough for the day's meat.

Each sunup there were new diversions planned: A bull and bear fight, when a grizzly was put into a great stockade along with a bull, and they fought it out while the interested audience took sides and cheered. Perhaps the victor was the bull, and old Bruin lay gouged, with entrails exposed to the sun, or Toro took defeat by being squeezed in powerful hairy arms until his very bones were crushed and life oozed away. Sometimes there was a riding contest, where horsemen were required to ride and carry trays of glasses filled to the very rim with wine. They galloped at breakneck speed, their gay red sashes flying in the wind, and then stopped suddenly to put down the tray without spilling a drop, while those who watched called out taunts, or the valley resounded to "Viva, vaquero! Bravo!"

And the tertulias, those evening get-togethers that often cost the host a thousand dollars for one night. Perfect dances they were with never a wallflower, for the master of ceremonies led each woman in turn to the dance floor and danced a few steps with her. There were folk dances with set figures and the new polka mazurka and other European round dances which traders and later colonists had introduced. The fandango was always a favorite dance with castanets and the one woman of a man's heart; then when the music stopped, a man must recite a verse, preferably something manufactured from his own wit. What a chance to show off before all. What an opportunity to pass a subtle dig about someone in the company, or a compliment that would make a señorita blush with her pride and love for you. Tables under ramadas (shelters made of green boughs) were piled with delicacies, and wine that had traveled days and days in carts drawn by ambling old oxen was poured fast as water.

The good God sent so many babies that there was always a name day to celebrate for a niña or niño, always another fiesta to come hard upon the last one and make life pleasant. For who would work among rancheros, when there were Indians? A Californian must keep his hands smooth, his mustache waxed, and his tongue sugary with compliments for the ladies. It took time and energy to think up original poems to have ready when the need came. Cattle grazed, grew, and were slaughtered while the ranchero took his ease. Each hacienda had many Indians to labor, and all were strictly specialists, five women or six to grind corn, several in the kitchen, and some to nurse the babies, some to sew and spin.

Padres were disturbed when Indian babies were taken from their mothers early so they would be trained properly. The children cried for their brown mothers, but eventually got over loneliness and became good maidservants. Indians were well-satisfied with a fathom of black, red, and white beads and enough ground corn to feed them for their season's work. Rancheros feeling righteous would say to padres who objected: "We stand as God-parents to them and teach the catechism and pay for their clothes and beads. We do as much as you did." And so life went on along the Salinas, with padres growing ever more feeble in their power over these children they had converted and enslaved, and many mission Indians, encouraged in their discontent by soldiers and colonists, were growing daily more restive under the padres.

At San Miguel the All-Seeing Eye, painted with such devotion by Esteban Munras, was still bright. It looked down on saddened faces. San Antonio was only a shadow of its former glory. "Taxes! Taxes! The mission system has failed!" That was the cry abroad these days.

Advance agents talked up secularization, and Indians listened eagerly to soldiers and colonists, who told them they would be free. But *freedom* to them meant no more work and mission stores to eat. Soldiers told them that friars were stealing from them. Colonists wanted secularization; they wanted Indian land and Indian labor. Governor José Figueroa encouraged the padres to let Indians run their own affairs. He issued an order for emancipation of Indians best fitted for freedom, with land, implements, and seed allotted to each, while the padres, powerless, had to stand by and see the fruits of freedom melt away from the childlike ones in vino and indolence, which ended only when Indians had to go and work for colonists in order to eat.

Feliciano Soberanes, ex-soldier and landed don of the Alisal, saw the mistake that Governor Figueroa had made in giving Indians their so-called liberty. He fought secularization with every weapon he knew. Don Feliciano was a portly man of forty-six, with eleven children and another on the way (thanks to God). He was a power in the Salinas and people listened to him. Feliciano's son Francisco was now twenty-five, and had a sizable family of his own; he too worked against secularization.

Hartnell, the English trader, agreed that the Indians would be lost without the guiding hands and heads of the padres, but the hardheaded Scot, David Spence, felt that Indians must skin their own snakes and sink or swim. Missions were past their usefulness now and failing; why prolong their death rattle?

Spence had no intentions of stirring up the governor against him for the sake of a few lazy Indians. Hadn't he said from the first that even a Scot could be a landed don in this new country? His father-in-law Estrada had taken the matter up with Governor Figueroa, and in spite of the growing resentment against Americanos and English holding land in California, the governor had promised to grant Rancho Encinal y Buena Esperanza to David Esteban Spence. The governor was canny and made stipulations to the Scot. He must build a house on the place and it must be habitable within the year to show his intentions as a citizen, not as a mere landholder. And when the property was confirmed the corners should be marked not by boundary stones but by planting some fruit trees, either wild or tame, and of some utility. Any violations of these and other conditions would cause Spence to forfeit his right to this fine land bordering the Salinas River and it could be given to another. Was he to take a chance and lose thousands of acres of land for Indians who hadn't enough sense to hang on to what they got? Besides, he now had a son three years old to consider and plan for.

At Christmas rain beat angrily against the whitewashed adobe walls of Our Lady of Solitude and howling wind lashed with bitter cold fingers at Indians who had come to be Wise Men who followed the Star in the beautiful Pastorela written long ago by the padre. The Star was there, a crude homemade affair shining among the green boughs of pine, and the altar was alight with tapers. But there were few to sing the sweet songs so dear to the padre's heart, and the mission was pitifully poor in worldly goods. Padres knew this was the last Christmas Mass; no more would voices be lifted in song at Mission Soledad. Orders had come that the missions were to be secularized, to be done away with. Heads bent in prayer to the Blessed Babe born in a stable long ago. Surely Christ Jesus would not forget those who had labored so lovingly and faithfully in the Salinas.

4

Two Suits of Underwear and a Horse

Hartnell, the English trader, bought 2,971 acres of the Alisal grant from the soldier Feliciano Soberanes, although the grant had not yet been confirmed. Don William moved his wife and family from Monterey to the Alisal for the summer, and then, evidently enchanted by this sheltered place in the country, decided to stay there. Perhaps the "English squire" in him was uppermost and the trader near forgotten in the pastoral beauty of Salinas Valley.

But the young wife Teresa liked fun and gaiety and loved to dance in spite of her almost continual "expecting." Gaiety must be brought to the Alisal if Teresa was to stay there. This was not hard in the early thirties when it was an easy day's travel from Monterey. Among the visitors was David Douglas, a Scotch gardener turned botanist, who stayed almost a year collecting plants and seeds. Indians called Douglas "Man of grass with nose harnessed," because he collected so avidly and wore glasses. During Douglas's stay Hartnell had an idea, a wonderful idea. He was a university man, a scholar, and here in this new country there was a need for dons' sons to be educated properly. Padre Short, the well-educated cleric, was called in for opinion and the three talked over Hartnell's great new scheme: a college in the Valley of the Salinas.

Douglas went on to the Sandwich Islands and Hartnell

planned his college, a great adobe building with dormitory and a master's room upstairs and study rooms downstairs and another structure for kitchen and eating place.

Patiently, brick by brick, Indian converts trained by mission padres labored to build El Colegio de San José so that an English trader could bring higher education to Spaniards and Mexicans and Californians. The first college in California was built and ready for students in January, 1834.

HARTNELL COLLEGE

Carefully written notices were sent out by Indian couriers to those fathers with likely boys, and two notices were printed in octopus ink on cartridge paper and tacked up in Monterey, the capital. One was on the Customs House where it would attract the attention of those with business in the building. The other was fastened to the corner of an adobe that acted as courtroom.

On these posters Don William P. Hartnell told all concerned about the new college. He would teach pupils Latin, French, German, writing of essays, mathematics, and philos-

ophy. There would be special attention to Christian doc-
trine and morals, and habits and manners. Each student was
required to have two suits of underwear, necessary top
clothes, and a horse. He must furnish his own carbon to
write with and a roll of cartridge paper to write upon. If
the student was wasteful with paper the college could not
undertake to furnish more since paper was hard come by.
The tuition was $200 a year.

Dons made rich by hides and tallow along the Salinas
and traders of Monterey stood in knots, shaking heads
and chuntering over this new idea, back in 1834. Boys would
only turn into softies studying such things as philosophy,
essay writing, and languages. Besides, if all young sons went
to writing essays who would manage ranchos and attend the
practical part of life? Education might be all right, but gold
would ease hunger when philosophy would only make the
belly lean and the head awhirl with ideas. El Colegio de San
José opened with fifteen pupils.

5

Prescription for Disappointed Lovers

THERE WERE no doctors in the whole long valley of the Salinas. Padres were clever with both fingers and herb dosing, but most settlers were at least twenty-five miles from any mission. Rancheros must depend upon Indian remedies and the old Spanish herbal printed in Cadiz, Spain, that was passed around from one family to another until its tattered pages were dimmed by age and hard usage. Finally General Vallejo had the book reprinted so that it could continue its usefulness to sojourners in this new country.

Perhaps a lover was jilted and the devil melancholia settled upon him. The cure was printed in the herbal. "Eat radishes and sugar, and place over the heart a poultice of the same in a cloth dyed with cochineal." There was even a prescription for sharpening the wits! "Powdered mustard well sifted and snuffed, in moderation though for the habit grows, will enable the user to comprehend more in an hour than others who do not know the remedy can comprehend in a day."

Toothache could be cured in no time. "Carry in the mouth the eyetooth of a man or that of a black dog." Chicken stewed in wine was a specific for catarrh.

Indians contributed medicines tested for generations. Suppurating wounds were quickly and painlessly cleansed in a most unusual way. A tiny cage was woven from twigs, and bluebottle flies were put inside it, then the cage was tied to the suppurating wound. When there was no pus to support maggots the wound was clean and healing began. Zauschneria, the little scarlet trumpet flower so bright on dry hills in summer, was called balsamea by those early settlers. In the form of a tea it was a mild but very efficient germicidal wash for eyes, skin, or any mucous membrane, and would cure the dread poison oak. Taken internally it cured ulcers of stomach or intestines.

Padres frequently reminded rancheros that the good God had blessed Californians by placing all necessary curatives right at their hand. Was not the sacred bark, cascara sagrada, good for bowels of man and beast, and growing in every canyon? And plumes of gray sage blowing in the wind were just waiting to be crushed and put on a bruise. There was chilicote root (wild cucumber) to be ground and fed to those who suffered pain, so that they would sleep and forget all agony, and tender young fern fiddles to stew for tapeworm, and yellow buttons of camomile for colic. What more could God provide?

A not too popular English ranchero made a great name for himself and in one brief moment blotted out all rancor against him. The young child of a Spaniard was very sick and wasting away. All remedies had been tried, but the child could keep no food down. In desperation the young mother ran out with the baby in her arms as the Englishman rode by along El Camino Real (The King's Highway). She begged him to help her—to do something so that her child would not join the almost continuous company of "little white funerals."

The Englishman got off his horse and went toward the newly whitewashed adobe house. Carefully with his knife he scraped off some whitewash, then with the handle of the same knife he ground it fine in the palm of his hand. This powder was mixed with a little water and administered to the baby. It stayed down! Stomach sweetened, the child was able to eat, and recovered. After that the Englishman's fame spread and he was called in frequently when there was a sick baby. The Salinas had her first baby specialist. Many years later he admitted he only used common sense and took a chance.

Surgery was simple in those days. Manuel Boronda, a ranchero and father-in-law to Feliciano Soberanes' son Francisco, was breaking wild colts. The obstreperous youngling ran between two scrub oaks and the result was a dangling broken leg for Manuel Boronda. The leg was of no use as it was, and feeling of it with gnarled brown hands the old man decided the bones were too mashed up to make a good "set."

"Bring a saw," he roared to a vaquero. "Give me a tumbler of whisky and go to work!"

The vaquero sawed. During the process of amputation the leg flew up so that Boronda claimed the distinction of being the only man in the world who had ever kicked his chest with his own toe. Herbs were put on the stump as a poultice to stanch the blood, and before long Manuel Boronda was hobbling around on a homemade wooden leg.

Manuel Boronda had another distinction, for he could be called the first experimental psychologist in the region. Through necessity, he invented a lie detector, simple and infallible and used on many occasions. This is the way it worked. One by one, all concerned were called into the room where the old man sat. On the table was placed a milk pan with an inch or two of water in it. Boronda had the suspect stick his finger in the pan and hold it there until all movement of water ceased. Then suddenly he asked, "Did you steal?"—or whatever the crime might be. The lips might say "no," but if the person was guilty he couldn't control the nerve reflex. The water moved! Rings from a quivering finger told the tale. If the person was innocent there was no reflex action.

Midwives were continually busy in the Salinas. There were always one or two Estradas, Soberanes, Malarins, or Hartnells about to come into the world. Besides, the midwife must attend the dead after the padre had gone, and see that jaws were tied up, a poultice of lime on the belly to keep it from swelling, and pennies on eyelids.

Death was an event along the Salinas, and mourners came from all the ranchos. The wake was important, and the turning out of an artistic corpse challenged the creative genius of a midwife.

The body was laid out on the table, and stiff lace curtains were draped like waterfalls to the floor. Candlesticks, as many as could be procured, were put at head and feet, and if the house was a proud and prosperous one and there was time, the midwife went to work cutting fancy paper frills to pin around candles and on the curtains.

First to the house of death came faithful mission Indians, who arrived at dawn and waited outside until just before sunrise, then silently they filed into the room and sang softly the chants for the dead that padres had taught them, ending the ceremony as the sun's first rays burst forth in glory from behind the mountains. Without a single word they went quietly away, their sweetly simple tribute paid to the dead.

Next came the mourners, whole families of them, babies and all, dusty and travel-weary from their trek and ready to attack with appetite the huge collation prepared by Indian servants.

After a decent interval and with proper deference for the dead, the homemade coffin was placed on an oxcart with wheels well soaped to keep it from creaking, and taken to the mission. Mourners followed on horseback and in carts. A padre said the Rosary, and then, after Mass, the body was put away in the cemetario of the mission, and another wooden cross was added to those marking faithful ones who had departed from the Valley of the Salinas.

6

The Last Matanza

DARKNESS. A padre's weary body coming slowly into consciousness for the work of a new day. Outside, restless unfamiliar voices and the uneasy bawling of cattle, as if the very beasts of the field knew a change was upon them this day. The rough gray robe made from mission-grown wool was comforting against crisp cold air, but heavy sandals were like ice on bare feet. Across the compound to where a few faithful Indians waited. Oh, God grant courage to a padre's heart, courage such as the Father of Missions had brought into the wilderness long ago! A voice raised in song! The canticle to the dawn!

> Now comes the dawn
> Brightening to the day
> Hail Mary Hail
> Let us all say.
>
> Comes morning light
> Brightening the day
> Amen Jesus
> Let us all say.

Already at San Antonio missionaries were gone and cattle had been slaughtered or divided up among Indians; Mariano Soberanes, ranchero and brother of Feliciano, was appointed comisionado over Indians who remained there.

The All-Seeing Eye at San Miguel looked down upon a deserted place where once there had been over a thousand neophytes laboring for the mission. There was not even a dipper to drink from at San Miguel, and already colonists had begun to take tiles from the very roof.

Padre Juan Cabot, who had given the best years of his life to San Miguel, still clung to the mission. He had been dickering with authorities over missions, to be allowed to keep the $808 which two years before had been paid, by W. E. P. Hartnell the trader, for mission goods. This would be enough to take him home to his beloved Spain. But word had come recently that he could retain only half that amount in payment for his work. This would not be enough to take him back to Spain, and where else could an unwanted penniless Spanish missionary go?

Our Lady of Solitude was to go down before progress, before those who had decided the mission system was a failure. Thousands of hides would be stripped from cattle raised at Soledad and shipped from Monterey in Spanish, English, and Americano boats. The best animals would be kept for breeding and given out to rancheros favored by those politicians in power; and Indians would have what was left to take to their land. These colonists were quick to forget that without the Cross to lead the way for soldiers, colonists, and politicians, settlement along the Salinas might have come too late for them to share in the spoils.

Padre Francisco Vicente de Sarria of Soledad knew well the doings of politicians. Hadn't he fought them when he followed in the footsteps of Junípero Serra as presidente of missions? Hadn't one after the other in the quick procession of governors wanted to do away with him, to banish him, because he had refused to swear allegiance to Mexico? Hadn't he lived within the walls of Soledad as a prisoner, constantly under arrest? Let them secularize the Mission of Our Lady of Solitude and take away all support and even the very cattle and implements, Francisco de Sarria would stay on with the handful of faithful Indians to share their food and their fate.

With sun up the dividing began; the slaughter started. Excited cries of Indians, happy to be free and treating the whole affair as a fiesta, were mingled with thousands of hoof-beats and bawling cattle. Yellow clouds of dust spread across the valley to choke up the nose and throat and to settle finally like yellow powdery snow on the little pink Roses of Castile which bloomed each year near the mission door, that they might serve on the altar of Our Lady.

Anxious greedy faces of rancheros watched those in authority divide the cattle, and black looks were exchanged when an especially fine bull was driven past them to go into the herd of another. Like buzzards they were, leaning against the split redwood fence waiting for the carcass of a dying mission. Some settlers didn't even bother to stop their haggling and loud protests and to come when the noonday bell rang for prayers; instead, they waited to share the beans and tortillas provided by Indians, at this last matanza.

The padre stayed on at Soledad month after month, dependent now upon a handful of faithful Indians and the goodness of heart in some rancheros. But even the nearest settlers lived miles away, and their memories were short. Some older Indians, worn out with a lifetime of labor in the Salinas, were laid away to rest at last in the cemetario behind the mission. Younger ones, left without the steadying influence of their elders, wandered away to work on ranchos.

Food grew ever more scarce at Soledad, and Sarria began to ail in body, but the spirit was strong. Devoted ones in his flock feared for him, and a runner was sent to fetch Jesus Maria Vasquez del Mercado, the priest who struggled on alone at San Antonio.

Padre Sarria mounted to the altar one day as usual to say Mass for the handful of Indians who were left in the crumbling Mission of Our Lady of Solitude. The good God sent unconsciousness to dull the senses of a starving one who served him with such high courage. Padre Sarria died with the chalice in his hand before the priest from San Antonio arrived.

Faithful Indians fashioned a litter, strapped together with rawhide thongs, and the padre was carried on their shoulders over miles of mountains to San Antonio. The last journey of Sarria was illumined by pine torches in the hands of grieving neophytes who hoped to spell off the litter bearers, but Sarria was "so light" that there was no need to share the precious burden.

The padre was laid at the epistle side (right) of the altar near the wall, with no monument to mark his coming or going save May flowers placed by loving Indian hands. Our Lady of Solitude was now left to bats and owls and weather.

7

"Out with the Gringos!"   1840

THERE WAS trouble along the Salinas, trouble that started on the very land where long ago De Anza and his colonists had camped on their way north.

Isaac Graham, a whisky distiller from Kentucky, had established a distillery at Natividad, the only settlement in the valley. This distillery was the magnet that drew a gang of trappers who came over the Sierras, and sailors who had jumped ship at Monterey. Outlaws of all kinds seemed to smell from afar the wheat mash, and head for Natividad and Isaac Graham. They drank and gambled and fought amongst themselves; and then, according to rancheros along the river, these ruffians stole what was loose and bothered native women.

Something must be done. There were now, according to Don W. E. P. Hartnell the census taker, twenty-seven men who owned ranchos in the district. Surely these men could demand that Mexico do something to protect the homes and rights of her decent citizens! The Soberanes, Castros, Estradas, and Malarins, and other Spanish and Mexican Californians along the river were worried. Was theirs to be the fate of Texas, where the same kind of patch-pants ruffians had drifted in until they were in the majority and had overthrown the Mexicans and grabbed the land for themselves?

Rancheros on the Salinas Plain were eager to be done with gringos. The military must act!

The military did act promptly, for there was the matter of politics. Governor Alvarado wanted home rule for California, and claimed the foreigners at Natividad were plotting to overthrow the government and take charge.

"We have welcomed you and treated you well," he told them. "You have taken our land and our lives as it pleased you, and you plot to take our country away from us. You say California is too big and fine a land for Mexicans, and that missions have lost their hold, and padres have trained Indians to work and raise cattle, and there's land waiting. You claim that Spaniards failed and Mexicans are shiftless, and Anglo-Saxons must rule America from sea to sea. We say: 'Out with the gringos!'"

Captain Castro, cousin to Feliciano Soberanes, was in charge of the roundup of all British and American aliens. They were to be seized, taken to El Castillo in Monterey, and held in prison until they could be shipped by boat to Tepic prison in Mexico. Even American and English travelers along El Camino Real were captured by mounted soldiers. Only those married to California women and those who were naturalized Mexican citizens could remain unmolested. This last must have eased anxiety of both Don David Spence and Don William E. P. Hartnell, who might well be thankful for time spent on the catechism.

There were over seventy men in the prison, and not even Thomas Oliver Larkin, the Bostonian consul at Monterey, could get them free before they sailed for Mexico!

The Salinas was cleared of Isaac Graham and his gang of ruffians, and rancheros settled back into the life of peace, ease, and begetting.

8

Granted to Soldiers, Colonists, and Traders—The Carcass

THE MISSIONS were no longer functioning, but the land was left. Governor Alvarado, whose wife Martina Castro was first cousin to Feliciano Soberanes, asked Soberanes in 1841 to take charge of Mission Soledad lands and the twenty Indians that were scattered around the vicinity of the mission, and to give them absolute freedom. He was to be in charge; a mayordomo and juez auxiliar (auxiliary judge), his jurisdiction extended to the Mission San Antonio which was in charge of his brother Mariano.

Perhaps because of this relationship with the Soberanes family, or because he felt that more land in the hands of established settlers would ensure plenty of defenders against invasion of either English or Americanos, Alvarado went on a granting spree in the valley of the Salinas.

Feliciano Soberanes, because he had helped Alvarado get rid of Isaac Graham and his gang, received Rancho San Lorenzo to the south, a grant of 21,884.38 acres. This was in addition to the Sausal 1,024 acres and Alisal 2,971 acres which Feliciano already owned. The ranchero could use all the land he could get with fourteen children to look out for.

Feliciano's eldest daughter Josefa, twenty-eight years old, received in the same year Rancho Los Coches, a grant of

8,794.02 acres, which was not far from Mission Soledad where her father was in charge.

Feliciano's son Francisco was claimant of the great Rancho Zanjón de Santa Rita (zanjón means deep ditch or

FELICIANO SOBERANES

drain). This rancho contained 48,823.84 acres and was granted in the same bountiful year of 1841 by Alvarado.

Nor was Mariano Soberanes, brother to Feliciano, neglected by the governor he had helped. He received two grants: the first was San Bernado Rancho granted June 16, 1841, and shared with a brother, Juan. This grant of 13,-345.65 acres of rich bottom land was far to the south end of the Valley of Salinas; then perhaps because he was in charge of scattered Indians around San Antonio, Mariano was granted Rancho Los Ojitos, a piece of 8,900 acres along the San Antonio River, where first the padres had settled, and where the herds of Mission San Antonio had once roamed.

It had paid the Soberanes family well to help Governor Alvarado with his fight againts the gringos. Altogether they now held 114,959.89 acres of land. The children, grandchildren, and great-grandchildren of the young soldier José Maria Soberanes, who had first come with Portola and married colonist Castro's Ana Josefa, were doing well by themselves, but they were to do still better in the land grab.

That other soldier, Estrada, and his descendants were not far behind. Rancho Santa Margarita of 17,000 acres, which had once been a part of Mission San Luis Obispo over the grade, was granted to Joaquin Estrada. This fine bottom land was where padres had first grown corn and vegetables. Then there was Asuncion, the place where padres had kept a storehouse for all missions in the Salinas, and had met to confess. That went to Pedro Estrada and consisted of 17,000 acres.

To Rafael Estrada the governor gave Rancho San Lucas, 8,874 acres. All this land in less than two years in addition to the ranchos Buena Vista and Llano Buena Vista, granted in 1823 to the Estrada family, making a grand total of well over a hundred thousand acres in this one family.

Don David Spence, the Scotch trader married to Adelaida Estrada, came in for his share from Alvarado. He was given another square league of land.

Juan Malarin, the Peruvian trader who married Adelaida's sister, was not faring badly in the take. He and his children had been granted Rancho Chualar (pigweed) and Rancho Zanjones and Rancho Guadalupe, three of the best pieces in the district, making up 24,469 acres. The Salinas was doing well by soldiers and traders who had first settled along her banks.

Then friction between home-rule minded Governor Alvarado and the military Governor Vallejo became so violent that Mexico resolved to unite civil and military power in one person. Both Vallejo and Alvarado were removed, and from Mexico came General Manuel Micheltorena. He arrived early in 1842 with his cholos (convict army), gathered from the streets of Mexico. They were practically naked, and dirty, and like savage Indians, and promptly went to work to "subdue" California.

A revolution broke out along the Salinas, when it was discovered that Governor Micheltorena and his convicts had joined forces with the sharpshooters of Isaac Graham, recently released from Tepic prison and now more active than ever. Micheltorena was also in with the Americanos that Captain John Sutter had mustered to the north. Micheltorena made it worth-while for Sutter and his band to help fight the Californians. He gave grants to Sutter in his New Helvetia, that made the land Alvarado had given along the Salinas seem mere token grants! Soon Sutter would own California.

The crafty two-faced General Micheltorena with his ragtag bobtail foreigners rode boldly through the Salinas, stopped at what was left of Our Lady of Solitude and demanded of administrator Feliciano Soberanes forty head of horses, fifty cattle, four yoke of oxen, and some sheep.

Soberanes complied, but demanded a receipt from the general, a slip of paper.

Micheltorena rode on south to enter into battle against Alvarado and Castro, who were the leaders of the loyal Californians. There were Americanos and English on both sides, and they promptly refused to fight when they met, leaving the Californians and Mexicans to fight it out.

Micheltorena and Alvarado clashed. The engagement

was mostly an artillery duel at Cahuenga Pass, for nobody took the chance at getting hurt. The Californians had four hundred men and two cannons against Micheltorena's three cannons. Casualties: one horse on the patriots' side, and on Micheltorena's side, a mule wounded.

Then Micheltorena capitulated! His cause was lost when the foreign riflemen he had recruited at great cost and with Sutter's help would not aid him. He agreed to leave Alta California, taking his cholos with him.

With Micheltorena's departure the last vestige of real Mexican rule was gone, and only shadowy allegiance to Mexico remained in the hearts of most Alta Californians. They were weary of the constant change of governors and of Mexican politics.

José Castro, a descendant of the original colonist, became the military commandante, and Pio Pico was made governor.

Before General Micheltorena left, Feliciano Soberanes demanded his eight hundred dollar payment for cattle, horses, oxen, and sheep but the bill was not paid.

Soberanes had an idea. The Mission San Miguel and its land had recently been sold by Governor Pio Pico to William Reed, an Englishman, and his partner, Petronillo Rios, for three hundred dollars. There was still Mission Soledad open for offers. Our Lady of Solitude even in the lean year of 1825 had been valued by tax collectors themselves at thirty-six thousand dollars.

Soberanes had his son-in-law draw up a petition to the new governor Pio Pico. He suggested that the amount owed him by the Mexican government would be canceled if the governor would grant him Mission Soledad' and its lands.

And so it was that Our Lady of Solitude with her 8,899.82 acres of fertile land and miles of irrigation ditches went to Feliciano Soberanes for forty horses, 50 head of cattle, four yoke of oxen, and some sheep!

Padre Sarria slept in peace at San Antonio, and chaff blew from the wheatfields that soon were up to the very walls of the brown adobe church of Soledad. Crows sat on the walls and cawed as the sun burst forth from behind the mountains soon after dawn.

PART V

Brush Jumpers and the Come-And-Get-It Era. 1845-1846

THE PANIC of 1837 in the Eastern United States was to be the indirect cause of great changes along the prosperous Salinas in 1845-1846, changes which were to alter lives of rancheros and breed hatreds to last for generations.

Americans and Californians around the Mexican capital at Monterey saw the handwriting on the wall. Mexico would not long be able to hold California, and the English already had eager eyes on this land of sunshine and plenty. It was *surprising* how much was known about California and her political troubles by Her Majesty's officials on ships at sea and on the tight rainy little isle itself!

Don David Spence, the Scotch trader, was said to be among those intriguing for a British protectorate in an underground way, while he kept friendly with American Consul Larkin, and remained a loyal Mexican subject married to a California woman.

The Americans were active too. Some rancheros in the Valley of the Salinas heard by grapevine that the Americano secretary of state, James Buchanan, had written secretly to Consul Larkin to take advantage of any Californian revolutionary movements against Mexico, and to encourage natives to work for home rule; then the Americans would ask the Californians to become a territory of the United States.

The expansionist, President Polk, wanted to grab California either by peaceful means or by war. But Thomas O. Larkin, the Bostonian consul at Monterey, was a canny man. He planned another way to outwit the English and gain California. There was safety and power in numbers, Larkin figured, so he sent letters east telling of the vast golden land of promise beside the Pacific, and its sunny climate, with warm winters and no snow to shovel, and thus was started the propaganda that was California's first publicity campaign.

Land-hungry adventurers, remittance men, and panic victims struggling on barren eastern farms read in the *North American Review* and other magazines and newspapers, especially in the New York *Sun*: "A 'foreigner' can become a citizen of California by obtaining 2 signatures to his petition. He then possesses the right to take up vacant land, and may secure as much as eleven square leagues upon payment of 26 dollars in fees. Many such grants held by such owners are 33 miles long by 3 miles wide."

John Charles Frémont, the illegitimate son of a runaway mother, and now an obscure lieutenant of topographical engineers, helped the cause. He had been sent by the United States War Department ostensibly to make maps of the province since no dependable map existed. Frémont had married the daughter of a senator and was in a position to get ahead if he could please the expansionist President Polk. With the aid of his wife, Frémont wrote two reports that painted California in romantic and glowing colors and himself as the hero.

In 1845-1846 Horace Greeley did not need to urge land grabbers to go west; those articles were enough. A large party of emigrants formed in Arkansas, Missouri, and Illinois. Many had been indentured people originally from Virginia.

Some were criminals. As many as seven thousand gathered at Independence, Missouri, and every person joining up was expected to be well-armed with rifle or heavy shotgun and sixteen pounds of powder or bullets. The Come-and-Get-It Era was on!

A few of these wanderers arrived in the Salinas Valley, and immediately things began to happen.

The second and third generation of land grantees, California natives, were prosperous, easygoing, and not used to the sharp ways of these new gringos who promptly had their petitions for citizenship signed, looked on all land as *government,* and claimed as their own any stray cattle that were unbranded. They moved Indians off fertile land into hill regions where they couldn't make a living, by giving them whisky, then offered these impoverished ones work. Christianized Indians were allowed to do housework and cattle riding. Gentile or wild Indians had to do menial work to live. Among these emigrants becoming Mexican citizens were Southerners. Were they going to bring black slaves here into the Valley of the Salinas?

Rancheros objected loudly against these new people who did not understand the ways of Californians and took advantage of customs of the country. These gringos didn't know that always since the days of the padres in the Salinas a Spanish Californian whose horse gave out would catch another and leave his. If hungry he would kill a beef, cook it, and eat it without thought of "repaying." He simply left the hide where the owner could find it easily. His neighbor did the same when in need. If a ranchero had a streak of hard luck there was always money in a trunk under the bed in the home of a friendly ranchero. "Go get what you need" were five words best known in the smiling valley. Malarins at Guadalupe were known to have forty thousand dollars in gold for all that needed it to help themselves.

Now, if a horse was exchanged, a man was called by

these gringos a horse thief! Americanos hanged men for cattle stealing when they were only doing what they had always done along the Salinas: "Take a marquerna" had always been the word. Two steers were tied together so they would drive well, for one animal alone would run all over the fields. A Salinas ranchero gave a steer to a person in need so that people could eat and *not* steal. When the needy man arrived home with his marquerna he loosed the animals and one steer wandered back to the rancho of its owner. The Estradas often gave a marquerna from the rancho Guadalupe, for beef raised there had the best flavor in the whole valley.

It was hard for Mexican and Indian minds to understand that taking cattle to eat was thieving, and, since there were no courts and the governor was final and supreme judge, the gringos took things in their own hands and didn't bother him. These hangings were called "healthy hangings," but they only brought things to a worse pass. The arma blanca (white weapon or knife) often came into play secretly and with dire results in hands of Mexicans and Indians.

These Yankee "brush jumpers" didn't understand that Indians burned down huts when fleas and lice were too bad, and built elsewhere. They grabbed the land the minute Indians moved.

Governor Pio Pico promptly had notices posted that Indians must stay on their land or lose it, but Indians couldn't read and gringos tore down the notices! Estradas, Soberanes, Castros, Borondas, and Hartnells rode through the valley to warn the Indians and tell them of the governor's notice. All was not well along the Salinas.

Hartnell's college had failed. There had been little interest in essay writing and morals and manners when so much land could be had for the asking! Sheep and cattle would grow hides and produce money. A knowledge of French and botany wasn't necessary to spend money, and morals and manners didn't matter much.

Josefa Soberanes had married a gringo, William B. Richardson, who had come to the Salinas from Maryland. Things were not going well. William and Josefa lived on her rancho, Los Coches, which Feliciano insisted should stay in her name —but Richardson liked his drink and was running up bills for liquor at the store of Rodriquez, while Josefa, big with her second child, stayed on the ranch to manage things and take care of her boy William.

Old Juan Malarin, the Peruvian trader, was having his troubles, too. Isabel, his first daughter, now twenty, had married an Estrada with land, a half brother of Governor Alvarado, but it was a different story with his daughter Maria. She had fallen in love with one of these no-good adventurers who had come into the valley. A Frenchman he was, named Bidache, a gambler and a tumbler from a circus! What *could* a common circus tumbler know about cattle or how to manage the inheritance which would someday be Maria's? Old Juan flatly refused to allow Maria even to see this Frenchman who spent his days in saloons at Natividad. But Bidache was getting back at old Juan. He was teaching Malarin's sons to gamble and lose money to him! Already Malarin could do nothing with his son Urbano, who was fast losing everything in this gambling fever that Bidache the French tumbler had brought into the Salinas. With ten children to keep track of and gringos all over the place squatting on a man's land, and then saying that no one had a right to so much land as these greasers owned, there was plenty of trouble. The old don was impatient for his son Mariano to return from Peru, where he was being educated as a lawyer.

Rancheros lived miles apart and could not protect each other from Yankee brush jumpers when these were out on "cow hunts," branding cattle belonging to rancheros, and, on the sly, making sheep's eyes at rancheros' daughters!

Ygnacio Pastor, an Indian who had received a little ranch at the Milpitas (little gardens) when the padres left, told that gringos were stealing fruit from the trees at San Antonio Mission.

A lone priest went to stay at San Antonio, which had been deserted in 1843, to try and keep these grabbing ones out and look after the ten or fifteen Indians left in the vicinity. San Antonio was the only mission in the Salinas not in ruins, this simply because it was too far away for people to cart things. The cattle were gone, and drink had ruined most of the Indians. Vines planted by padres whose bones long moldered in the soil of the Salinas were still bearing well. Fruit trees irrigated by the padres' ditches were loaded with fruit that gringos stole. A greaser priest would protect the place from these vandals as long as he could.

Then things came to such a pass that rancheros along the Salinas "broke out" and demanded that the Mexican government take measures against this Americano immigration that had poured into the country. Pio Pico, the governor of the province, received instructions from Mexico City to drive out all foreigners who were not licensed to hold land, but he did nothing to enforce the law.

"Consul Larkin has been flattering Pio Pico!" rancheros cried angrily. "Our own governor is deceiving us. Larkin is a smart Americano, and Pio Pico goes to parties at Larkin's house."

Matters grew worse in January, 1846, when Lieutenant John C. Frémont, the Yankee topographer, arrived in Monterey. He was a "foreigner" who had made trouble before in California, with his mountainmen. They had taken horses and killed Indians to the north. Had Frémont come to start war? It was well-known that this lieutenant had left sixty-two men with arms in the Sacramento Valley and had already bragged that California would not be hard to take, for its people were only a helpless handful of lazy, easygoing rancheros! He was not looked upon with friendly eyes by troubled rancheros.

Frémont must explain. All Salinas Valley land grantees who had homes in Monterey waited anxiously that day, while Frémont went with Consul Larkin to see Mexican Prefect Manuel Castro.

Castro asked what business a United States military man with soldiers at his disposal had in these parts.

Frémont told that he was engaged in a scientific survey of trade routes to the Pacific coast and his men were not soldiers at all, but scouts. Had not Castro heard of Kit Carson and Joe Walker, the well-known scouts who were now part of his company? He only wanted to pass the winter in California and leave for Oregon in the spring. He also wanted to purchase supplies in California.

This man Frémont sounded honest and harmless, so another Castro, Don José, the military comandante, gave permission to Frémont with the understanding that the exploring party was not to enter into any of the settlements of the country.

Frémont gave his word and then went along the Valley of the Salinas with a scout. He needed horses and mules, so he purchased from Indians 187 mules and horses that had once been part of mission stock. For each animal the Yankee topographer paid one string of beads and a butcher knife; then he returned to the Sacramento. Rancheros in the Salinas breathed more easily, but not for long.

On March 3rd, when new spring green was lush on the hills above the Salinas, the children of Don William E. P. Hartnell saw a cavalcade of soldiers riding up to their hacienda on Rancho Alisal. Frémont and his men were upon them again. He had broken the promise given to General Castro that he would not enter the settlements!

A rider was dispatched with this news to Consul Larkin, and word came back that Frémont had better come to Monterey. Frémont ignored this and announced that he intended to spend spring among the wild flowers of the Salinas. He said that he would move to the bank of the Salinas River that night.

But Frémont's "scouts," turned soldiers, were men who had been long without women, and Natividad, the only settlement in the Salinas, was not far away.

PART VI

A Woman Brought It On

Fat on the Fire

BEFORE many hours passed fat was in a fire that burned hot as hades itself. Three of Frémont's soldiers had gone to the house of Don Angel Castro, aged uncle of General Castro, the military comandante, and offered insult to one of the old don's beautiful daughters. Angel Castro was a Spaniard who had served his King and he had a fiery temper. He struggled to protect the girl, even attempting to wrestle with one of the drunken soldiers, the most insulting of the three. One soldier drew a gun, but even this did not quiet the aged don who was still a brave old warrior. The other daughters were frightened over the turn of events and screamed. The soldiers retreated, roaring drunken threats at the old man. They promised to return and "fix him."

The next day a courier rode through the wild oats three feet high on Rancho Alisal, to complain to Frémont, and little Sylvester Hartnell stood by saucer-eyed when the Californian asked Frémont to "return with your people out of the limits of this territory." Frémont the braggart merely shrugged his shoulders and the young courier rode away with hatred blazing in his eyes. In no time another courier came to Frémont with a letter from Prefect Manuel Castro:

Prefecture of the District
Monterey, March 5, 1846

Señor Captain J. C. Fremont:

I have learned with much dissatisfaction that in contempt of the laws and authorities of the Mexican Republic, you have entered towns of the district under my charge, with an armed force which the government of your nation must have placed under your command for the sole purpose of examining its own territory.

That this prefecture orders you immediately on receipt of this communication to withdraw from the limits of this department, with the understanding that if you do not comply, this prefecture will take the measures necessary to compel you to respect this determination.

God and Liberty
MANUEL CASTRO,
Prefect of Second District

Frémont went into a lather of temperament then. No greasers would tell *him* what to do!

Hartnell, who was on the rancho, begged Frémont to keep cool and follow orders, for Californians along the Salinas Valley were incensed over the treatment they had received at the hands of Frémont's men.

Consul Larkin sent a message from Monterey, urging Frémont to be circumspect.

But Frémont was belligerent and his men were out after greasers. He didn't even read Larkin's letter, for brag swelled him like a puff adder. He moved quickly up the hill behind Rancho Alisal to the very top of Gabilan Peak (Hawk's Peak), set up a breastwork of logs which he cut from Hartnell's land, nailed the Stars and Stripes to a pole and prepared for battle. Then he sent a letter to Larkin:

If we are unjustly attacked we will fight to extremity, and refuse quarter, trusting our country to avenge our death. If we are hemmed in and assaulted here, we will die every man of us, under the flag of our country.

Hartnell tried to reason with this self-styled martyr, and explain that no one had attacked him. He had been asked to leave because he had lied about his intentions and broken the promise to Mexican officials that he would stay out of settlements, and what was worse he had condoned the behavior of three drunken soldiers who had insulted women of the country. Hartnell repeated, no one cared to kill him. They wanted him out!

When Old Glory went up on the Gabilan above Hartnell's house just five days after Frémont had arrived in the valley, Castros, Soberanes, Estradas, Malarins, and others were up in arms over this gringo interloper.

Consul Larkin begged the Californian military comandante General Castro not to get rough, but to talk things over, and then he hastily asked in Washington for a man-of-war to come into Monterey Bay and to urge all concerned to dampen their powder.

But an insult had come to a woman within Don José Castro's own family. The gringos must go! Quickly the general sent proclamations out along the Salinas Valley, declaring that Frémont and his men were highwaymen who had dared to raise the American flag in defiance of the authorities. In no time Castro had raised two hundred men for his militia which he paraded within sight of the spyglasses on Gabilan Peak!

The ruse worked. For three days Frémont and his men waited and watched and then the flagpole fell. Those who were likely to be starved out and then, when they came down, finished by means of the arma blanca of Californians hidden in mustard and oats, decided they had done enough for the honor of their country. Frémont lost in his gamble for greatness! Quietly in the night he took his men back to the Sacramento, and spring flowers in the Salinas bloomed on, untrampled by this band of gringo thieves and rapers.

General Castro was filled with great good nature. He had fought a war and won it without a drop of California blood being shed. But the fiestas in celebration of victory lacked their usual wholehearted gaiety. What was to become of California? Pio Pico, the governor, and General Castro were constantly at sword's points over the division of the provincial revenues. Debts were pressing and soldiers pared down to almost nothing. Pico could command legislation favoring the civil instead of General Castro and the military. But Castro had his power too, for he was in control of the funds. And now to cap everything word had come from Mexico City that Paredes, the president of Mexico, had offered to transfer California to Great Britain as security for a loan.

War, 1846

WHITE-LATHERED HORSES raced in hot July sun over brown hills and into the Valley of the Salinas.

War! War was declared between Mexico and the Americanos! A frigate with a gringo commodore had sailed into Monterey harbor and hoisted the American flag in place of the Mexican flag on the Custom House pole. Gringos were in possession of Monterey!

General Castro and Pio Pico had letters from Americano Commodore Sloat, riders told breathlessly. He demanded surrender of troops, ammunition, and all public properties. Sloat said that if these were surrendered there would be no loss of Mexican life. He wanted General Castro and Pio Pico to meet with him and talk, and promised their lives and liberty would not be endangered. But Frémont had promised to stay out of settlements and had broken his promise.

Pio Pico refused to answer the gringo commodore; instead, he called a meeting of the Provincial Assembly. Eyes rolled and muscles twitched with excitement as these messengers re-created the Californians' hissing and cursing the gringos at that meeting. General Castro was already mustering troops. All men must be ready to fight to oust the invaders.

Womenfolk along the Salinas remembered other gringo

troubles. They pulled their shawls close, crossed themselves, and prayed that the Blessed Mother would remember the heartaches of all mothers and save their sons and brothers and husbands from being killed at war.

In a week another commodore of the gringos, Stockton, came to Monterey in a boat and before long Sloat, who claimed to be sick, turned his command over to Stockton and sailed away.

With Stockton came *real* trouble, for Frémont the highwayman was back, a major now in the Americanos' army, and left in charge of operations at Monterey!

"Fight the gringos!" The cry was echoed and re-echoed in each ranch house of the valley, and men began to sharpen their knives. Gringos may have Monterey, but Monterey was not the Salinas Valley!

But gathering and training Mexicans and Californians in the way of battle took time, and meanwhile men under Frémont were insulting to Englishmen and Americanos, who were Mexican citizens, as well as to the Californians themselves. They demanded cattle to feed their troops and gave in exchange only a scrap of paper. Sometimes they took horses without even giving a paper. Bitterness grew into seething hatred.

Not until nearly four months later, when autumn brown was on the hills and the wide plain, did a real battle with the gringos occur in the Salinas.

Frémont sent troops out boldly. At Natividad on the same ground where Isaac Graham and his men were taken, and where long before De Anza and his colonists had camped, they met the Californians led by General José Castro, a descendant of one of those colonists.

Frémont's sixty soldiers with plenty of firearms and ammunition were matched against eighty Californians who had only rawhide riatas and knives. But General Castro's men were better horsemen than las gamusas (the buckskins) led

by the gringo Captain Burroughs; besides, General Castro
had a trick up his sleeve.

Part of the Californians put spurs to horses and pre-
tended to race away in flight when Burroughs roared up on
his charger Sacramento. The gringos took after them, then
Castro's men turned on their pursuers with lassos, as they
came full speed through the tall growth of dried mustard.
At the same time some thirty Californians left behind rushed
up to attack the rear of Captain Burroughs. Lassos flew
through the air faster than Americano bullets. A pull, a
choking sound, then the quick flash of a knife, and silence.
Captain Burroughs fell dead from his horse, leading the
charge, an unloaded rifle in his hand. Five others were soon
killed. The fight lasted about half an hour. Gringos ran
through the dried mustard stalks and climbed oaks for safety,
Californians hot after them swinging riatas and shouting
for vengeance!

Then Captain Thompson, in charge but wounded, with-
drew his forces to care for his six wounded and to bury the
dead. The Battle of Natividad was over. Once more was
General José Castro victorious. Gringo invaders had learned
that the Valley of the Salinas was an unhealthy place for
them.

By the end of November, Frémont had his fill of the
region and he started south along the valley with his four
hundred and fifty men and several cannons, plundering and
burning as he went. At Mariano Soberanes' Rancho Los
Ojitos, horses and cattle were taken and the place burned,
because Soberanes had been loyal and helped the Californians. At Rancho Chualar, Francisco Estrada was arrested
for his part in the Battle of Natividad.

But the Salinas had not finished with Frémont and his
men. November was a wet month that year; winter rains
had set in with a fury. The river was high and quicksand
dangerous. Feed for animals was scarce and the beasts were so

weak that cannons were moved with great difficulty through gluey yellow mud. On they labored; each day took its toll of mules and horses, until, by the time they reached the head of the Salinas, soldiers had to drag the cannons. Up over the hill they went on El Camino Real where long ago weary explorers in the wilderness had come down into the valley sowing the mustard seed that was to help in the defeat of gringo invaders. The Salinas had seen the last of Frémont.

The next January (1847), Pio Pico and Frémont signed a treaty of peace, Mexico ceding California to United States for $15,000,000. But that treaty meant nothing to rancheros along the river.

There was only Santiago Estrada at Buena Vista and Don Antonio Maria Lugo living in the valley between Buena Vista and Soledad Mission, and five or six other rancheros nearer the river's mouth, but *they* had signed no treaty with the gringos.

"So the Mexicans have sold California to the Americanos for fifteen million and thrown us natives into the bargain!" roared Don Antonio Lugo. It was well-known now in the Salinas that the British had turned down the deal with Mexico for California because they realized the Americans were already on the ground. "I don't see how Mexicans could sell what they never had," the old don roared on, "for since the time of the king we sent back every governor they ever sent here. With the last, Micheltorena, they sent three hundred soldiers to keep us in order, but we sent *him* and his rag-amuffins back too." Don Antonio swore *he* would be no gringo citizen!

Juan de Mata Boronda, a relative of Francisco Sobanes' wife, carried on the war by himself. He got friendly with Americanos and talked to them about those "damned greasers," learned their habits, and then stabbed unsuspecting Americanos at night on their way home.

Esteban Munras, grantee of Rancho San Vicente and

painter of the All-Seeing Eye that looked down as Frémont's men passed San Miguel, said he didn't much care who took over, English or Yankees, now that the affair was settled and the disgusting Mexican politics over California were at an end.

But after the war the United States was too busy with its own politics to bother with political troubles in California. Instead of giving at once some form of territorial government, Congress entered into a fierce fight over the slavery problem. There had been talk in Washington of dividing California by making a line south of Monterey, where slavery might be established, the rest to be free. Part of the Salinas would be in the slavery belt, and part would be free.

Things grew strained. Americans came into the Salinas and felt they were entitled to land. They found large tracts occupied by Mexicans. This was not right. No man had a right to fifty thousand acres. Hadn't they fought for the country and the land? Land came with conquest. Squatters formed an association and made laws of their own, and granted to each member the right to a hundred and sixty acres of any land that was vacant or that they chose to decide was vacant! Mexicans resented this, and violently distrusted the government. There was constant trouble with words and with knives!

The gringos had posted proclamations saying that Mexican citizens would be given opportunity to become American citizens, or if they didn't choose to comply with the laws of the country, they would be given two years in which to dispose of their property and interests and get out. Many Californians were already selling their holdings to English and Americans and preparing to leave the province forever. They would have naught to do with this cutthroat government. Hartnell, Spence, and many others did all they could to promote friendliness and peace in the district, while they waited impatiently for a new territorial government to be formed.

In July, 1847, the Americano Company F gave a ball with supper and champagne at Mr. W. E. P. Hartnell's town house in Monterey. General Sherman, Lieutenant Henry Halleck, and Ord were at the party, and Estradas, Soberanes, Malarins, and many other old families with grants along the Salinas were invited. Very few Californians accepted. The gringos were celebrating the anniversary of the taking of California. They were offering insult by inviting Californians to watch them celebrate their conquest.

Then came word of Frémont's arrest at Fort Leavenworth. He was charged with mutiny, disobedience of commands of a superior officer, and a court-martial ordered to try him. He was found guilty and dismissed from the service.

There was great rejoicing along the Salinas; rancheros now felt more confidence in the new gringo government. These people were not all rapers and highbinders. El Capitán Frémont who had stolen gold earrings from the señoritas was receiving his just deserts at the hands of his own people. His rashness at Gabilan had been his undoing. There was such a thing as justice even in the souls of gringos.

In Washington the Cabinet finally took steps to try to force Congress to do something to secure a government for the newly acquired land of California, and rancheros in the smiling valley went about their peacetime occupation of spreading a thick carpet of golden wheat ears in an enclosure for horses to tread out. A big crop this year, plenty of tortillas, and time now for name-day fiestas!

Gold and Massacre in the Salinas, 1849

EASYGOING pursuits and the hide and tallow business were suddenly interrupted in the Salinas. To the north, gold had been discovered. In only seven weeks $76,866 had been taken out by one man and his Indians.

William Reed, the English sailor who had bought Mission San Miguel for three hundred dollars and was running a store, left his Indian wife and went with his partner Petronillo Rios to the gold fields. He led the procession. Many other Mexicans and Indians who knew how to pan gold in a batea, or wooden bowl, followed as fast as feet could take them. A widow loaded pans and pots on two donkeys and started for the mines to make her fortune cooking. In no time at all there was hardly a good vaquero left to ride range or an Indian with ambition enough to work in the fields of the valley.

The winter of 1849 was the wettest in years. Rain came down for weeks on end; the river swelled and washed away miles of good land, and the quicksand beds were enlarged, but that didn't dampen the ardor of gold seekers.

Night and day men traveled along El Camino Real to the mines. Men from Sonora in Mexico, men from the South and the East in a steady procession. They entered the Salinas through side valleys, as well as over the high pass that Portola's explorers had traveled so long before.

They stole horses and mules and killed cattle to eat all along the valley. Even at out-of-the-way and forgotten San Antonio Mission, which was the only mission not sold, Señor Gomez, who had been left in charge by a priest, complained of Sonorans stealing fruit from the trees that padres had planted. He grew tired of living there alone and fighting with marauders to protect the place for a few Indians, and he went away.

Word came back from the mines of bitter clashes with the Americanos who were not used to mining and who resented the Mexicans and patient Chinese who had come in to work. Peons, Chinese, and Mexicans were hanged without explanation and it often turned out that the wrong man had been hanged. People calling themselves vigilantes organized, but they were a mob who lawlessly tried to force lawless people! Over two thousand persons were killed in a few months.

Food was high too, the gold seekers wrote back. On the top of dry mountains where nothing would grow and there was so little water that even a drink was worth gold, onions were like nuggets and potatoes worth a pokeful of yellow dust. Hungry men gambled at poker for a mess of potatoes and some were even shot for trying to steal *one*. Beef was priceless and candles sold at a dollar each. Rancheros in the Salinas killed cattle off fast and shipped beef and candles. Then Americanos in the mines began crying for butter.

Old families along the river, with comfort and ease in mind, figured a way to share in the discovery of gold and not leave their ranchos for others to loot. They roped wild calves and colts and strapped kegs of cream to their backs with rawhide thongs; then these ease-loving ones sat in the shade of ramdas drinking vino and visiting while the creatures bucked until weary. Then they removed the kegs and took out the butter. Let the gringos sweat and grovel in the heat for gold and pay through their noses for butter.

The golden luxury went by wooden-wheeled oxcart to Monterey where it was shipped by boat to San Francisco and thence up the Sacramento, and finally pulled by mule team to the mines, while rancheros in the Salinas Valley went to Mass, welcomed more babies, and attended fiestas.

There were other changes in the district besides those brought on by the discovery of gold in 1849.

A newly made grave in the cemetario told where they had laid the old Peruvian trader Juan Malarin. That in itself would bring many changes to the valley, for there were ten children involved in the estate. The old don's son Mariano, educated in Peru as a lawyer, was to be administrator of the three great ranchos, Buena Vista, Guadalupe, and Chualar; but rancheros reminded one another that Mariano's mother was an Estrada, and the Estradas were noted for not knowing the value of money. The widow was to have half and the rest divided among the ten. The wind carried tales up the valley, and from as far as Monterey, about how fast that estate would go now that it was in younger hands. The Malarin girls would bring plenty of land along with their good looks to the husbands they picked out. Isabel Malarin at fifteen was already married to Rafael Estrada, her cousin. "With Estradas on both sides, well—" Heads shook and shoulders shrugged.

Then there was the Scotch salter, David Spence. He had given up his Monterey mercantile business in order to have enough time to manage his great holdings in the Valley of the Salinas. The dream of long ago was complete now, with the handle "don" in front of his name, and his only son David at school in Honolulu along with Pachecos and the sons of other landed California grantees. The boy had claim, through his mother's Estrada, to as good a Spanish California ancestry as the best of them!

What if he, Don David Spence, *was* called close and not too popular? A man who minds his money always has a good friend. Sticks and stones might hurt but words broke no bones. He thought back on the bleak days of his childhood in Scotland and was thankful. There was many a close Scot on the scrubby niggling heath that would give half his life to find himself a Scotch don owning miles of fertile land in the sunny Salinas.

DAVID ESTEBAN SPENCE

Feliciano Soberanes had sold his part of the Alisal Rancho to Governor Alvarado, who had taken tiles from the mission at Soledad for the roof of an adobe where he planned a summer home. Feliciano had built a fine house on the hill in Monterey, and would now go for only part of the summer to look over his ranchos in the Salinas. There was plenty for all his children and their children in the fertile Salinas.

The greatest change of all was the meeting of men at Monterey to draw up the first constitution for California. Californians and Americanos alike were to have a part in making of laws.

W. E. P. Hartnell, the English trader and ex-schoolmaster married to Teresa de la Guerra, and now with a houseful of children to his credit, was chosen as translator to the constitutional convention.

There was much to accomplish and several issues caused bitter warfare among the delegates, but on *one* question they were all agreed: no banks! Stories of the misery and ruin and destruction during the Panic of 1837 were still fresh in their memories and members were unanimous against the establishment of a banking system in California. Instead, they tried to figure out a way to prohibit the formation of corporations or a bank of issue without hampering business. What did it matter that gold dust, gold coins, Spanish doubloons, Mexican silver dollars, pesetas, reales, rupees, and even German coins were exchanged far above their worth, until bankers decided to accept them at bullion value?

Then there was the slavery business rearing its ugly head. Some at the convention claimed that the war with Mexico had deliberately been brought on by the Polk administration to get territory in which southern planters could find fields of employment for their slaves and territory out of which to form new slave states.

Already Southerners were at the mines with their slaves who didn't know they were in a free land. The blacks worked for their masters and saved what little they could scrape together to pay for their freedom. A tale had come to the Salinas of one slave who had a can of gold dust, and the master kept taking a little out, so that the man had to work twice as long to pay for his freedom, and when the papers finally came the master stole them and the slave worked again for his freedom. The man eventually freed himself once more, only to find too late that he had been free all the time. The black put on white clothes and "hanted" the master until the man went crazy in a little dry gulch up near the mines.

W. E. Shannon got to his feet in the convention and proposed an amendment to the constitution of California that: "Neither slavery nor involuntary servitude, unless for the punishment of crime, shall ever be tolerated in California." This was adopted unanimously, and so it was that several rancheros from the Salinas Valley sitting in convention had the privilege of adding their voices to create California the first slave-free territory of the Union! But once adopted, they were afraid this very clause would keep California out of the Union. She *could* be refused.

There was also the problem of color. Some states already in the Union were refusing admittance to people with dark skins and there were many Californians with Indian or Negro blood. There could be no refusal of dark-skinned folk in California as some gringo members suggested!

Tact and great diplomacy were necessary to get over this last hurdle. Hard looks and eyes glistening with anger were evident on all sides when the matter of color came up. California was to be free in every sense of the word. She was created free in that first convention.

The gold fields gave grudgingly to William Reed of San Miguel Mission and his partner, Petronillo Rios. Rios constantly reminded his sailor partner how much better they would have been in the Salinas, grazing cattle and carrying on their general merchandise store at San Miguel.

"We were doing a good trade with miners coming through and headed for the San Joaquin gold fields. Prices were high. It was better than this sweating," Rios complained.

But Reed was a proud Britisher and he hung on and on. Others had struck it rich; their turn might come any day.

In the meantime he bragged with the best of them. *He* had gold. Sacks of it.

"Don't do that," Rios begged. "Here we are among a lot of wild fellows. They may cut our throats."

Finally even El Piloto Reed grew tired of scarce food and so much hard work for so little gold. They packed pans and pots on their burros and returned to the Valley of the Salinas with what gold they had, to pick up life where they had left it.

Petronillo Rios went to stay on his rancho to the south of San Miguel, and Reed ran the store in a part of the mission where once missionary padres had sat around the fire on cold winter nights when the wind howled up the valley.

Then one evening about dusk, the brag of an Englishman caught up with him. On their way south, three miners Reed had known in the mines came into his place for meat and drink. They were surprised to see him behind the counter. Had he failed at the mines?

Reed smiled indulgently at them and pointed to the eight-year-old brother of his Indian wife. "I have plenty of gold. That little chap can't lift even the smallest bag!"

The miners didn't hurry. They had more to drink, and finally put down twenty dollar gold pieces to pay.

Reed, the show-off, to make good his brag went into the bedroom, got his only bag of gold and weighed out the change. Then they all had another drink on the house.

One of the miners, seeing the fire was low, went out to get wood and came back with an ax hidden among the logs he carried! A quick sure stroke and Reed went down where he was chatting. With that ax stroke, fear and greed turned all three miners into maniacs! They rushed into the bedroom where the "expectant" Mrs. Reed with an old midwife and the midwife's daughter and child were getting ready for bed. Mrs. Reed's head was split open before she could scream. The midwife's daughter fell next. The toothless crone grabbed a heavy stick to protect herself and her grandchild, but she had little strength and the killers made short work of her and the child. Reed's three-year-old son was snatched from the bed, held by the feet, and his head bashed against the thick adobe wall until it cracked like an egg. In the kitchen, a Negro was murdered as he slept. A sheepherder and his grandson were knifed in another room.

The murderers pulled the place to pieces in their search for gold dust, and dragged the bodies of their victims into one room where they planned to burn them. Then they discovered a child hiding behind boxes in the corridor. Mrs. Reed's eight-year-old brother had been friendly with them all evening. Pitifully he begged for his life.

One, perhaps a father himself, shoved the little fellow down again, as if to spare him, but other eyes were too sharp. "What is that you're hiding there?" The words were fraught with fear. "You want the brat to betray us?"

The boy was dashed to his death against one of the corridor pillars built so painstakingly by padres and Indians.

Daybreak at Mission San Miguel. Outside meadow larks on the fence posts sang their canticle to the rising sun. The miners ran out of the cloister toward the deserted church where the All-Seeing Eye of Esteban Munras looked down upon them as they tore the very doors of the church from their hinges. These maniacs used the doors that once had opened wide to welcome converts as a barrier to prevent anyone from entering the room where their victims lay in a bloody pile. But time was too short for a funeral pyre. The day was bright with sun and any minute an early traveler might pass by.

The terrified eyes of a child watched the murderers hurry to the corral for horses and ride away to the south, sure that they had left no living witness to their massacre.

A tiny frightened baby came from behind a great chest,

and little legs raced through the tall mustard in a short cut to the nearest rancho, which was miles away. But at four it was easy to get lost in mustard fifteen feet high.

Two days later Captain Pryce, of Los Osos Rancho, and a friend rode past San Miguel on their way home from San Francisco. There was nobody about and the sun was high. Restless cattle bawled in the corrals and doors were gone from the church.

Pryce rapped sharply on Reed's window. There was no answer. A premonition of trouble made the captain push

MISSION SAN MIGUEL

open the shutter. Things were all tumbled about. Trunks were emptied. There was blood on the floor. The place was a shambles. Without going inside the two men put spurs to their horses and raced to the rancho of Petronillo Rios and he in turn sent a rider over the grade to San Luis Obispo for officers.

Hearing the disturbance, an Indian handed Rios an earring he had found at a camp on Rios's own place, where traveling miners had stayed only the night before. Rios recognized the ornament as one of a pair he had seen in Mrs. Reed's ears.

Officers were ordered to shoot at sight. The murderers were obliged to travel by road, for they didn't know the country.

At last near the coast the maniacs were overtaken and two of them plugged on the spot. The third, an Irishman, surrendered and begged to be allowed to confess. He told the gory tale of wholesale murder, and how they found so little gold at Reed's that they planned to kill Petronillo Rios also, but there were too many Indians about the rancho and they were afraid. The Irishman was shot later in Santa Barbara.

There was blood of children on the walls of the padre's quarters at San Miguel, and the floor was stained black with the blood of a braggart. But one child was missing from the pile of corpses.

To the north a great circle of buzzards was black against the sky and in the tall mustard scarlet-winged black-birds scolded. Riders found a terrified lost child who lived long enough to tell his horrible story and then forget his troubles forever.

A bag of gold from the Sierras had brought a massacre to the Salinas!

OLD OVEN, MISSION SAN MIGUEL

PART VII

Horse Thieves and the Land Fight

Squatters

MANY OTHERS beside William Reed were disappointed in the mines. Some of these disillusioned creatures sifted into the Salinas Valley and squatted on land. They were so impoverished that they walked with sacks tied around their feet, long ago having lost the animals with which they had begun their travels. These were the remnants of the fifty to one hundred thousand people who had come in the great migration for gold, and they made constant trouble for rancheros. Spanish and Mexican grants meant nothing to these desperate gringos. Here was vacant land; try to get them off!

In 1850, after California was admitted to the Union, the Castros, Soberanes, Malarins, Estradas, and many other Californians brought pressure to have Washington send a lawyer skilled in Spanish colonial titles to get information and examine the disputed titles. William Carey Jones was sent and found the titles correct and equivalent to patents from the United States government. But this fact did not in any way alter the minds of squatters who constantly built their shacks on granted lands.

Don David Spence now the proud prefect of the District of Monterey appointed William Hartnell justice of the peace of the Alisal and Salinas Plain. Hartnell had his hands full trying to settle disputes in the valley. Finally, in desperation a United States Land Commission was set up, before which every claimant under Spanish and Mexican title must within two years present his claim with documentary evidence. Either the squatter or the grantee might appeal to the district court and from its decision to the Supreme Court. All lands for which claims were rejected were to be regarded as public domain.

Spanish-speaking Californian rancheros along the Salinas were desperate and bewildered. The United States treaty signed at Guadalupe Hidalgo had promised protection to Mexican and Spanish Californians. Didn't it amount to the same thing as confiscation of land for a ranchero to have to defend his title in three courts? A decent citizen who had owned land for years and years must now go into a foreign court and fight for his land in a strange language, while Americano squatters who had just come and settled on the land had equal rights in the courts, besides the advantage of speaking the language.

Shyster lawyers, realizing the helplessness of these Californians and the fact that there would be long-drawn-out court actions with golden California lands as the prize, rushed in from all directions and prepared for a field day. The great California land fight was on. No longer could an easygoing ranchero go by the old way of claiming land as it was written in "expedientes," that he owned "as far as eye could see and cattle could roam" from a certain point of vantage. These gringos didn't go by Spanish rules.

Helpless Indians were moved off land where they had scraped a living, and no provision was made for them. They tried stealing, sheep shearing, haying, or any other fair means or foul by which they could eat. No longer could rancheros make a pleasant home for them.

Some smaller rancheros, realizing that it would take years and all they had to fight in the courts, went down to defeat. They gave up their land, sold their cattle, and prepared to take what work they could do to live. Others, including Feliciano Soberanes, willingly agreed to give half of their land to lawyers in order to gain title and be free from squatters constantly declaring that the land was theirs.

The price of a free title was high, and meant that part of the beautiful San Lorenzo Rancho must go, where now

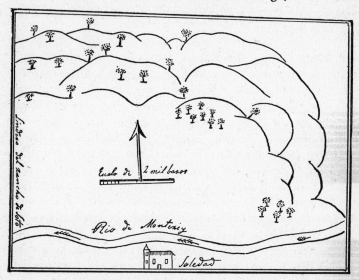

MAP BY ESTEBAN MUNRAS OF AN ADDITION TO RANCHO SAN VICENTE

one of Feliciano's sons was living, and land must go at Mission Soledad, land must go from each grant. The less land, the fewer cattle, the harder to manage.

Soberanes wished he could be as easygoing about it as were the Estrades all along the valley. Don Joaquin Estrada at Asuncion drank and made merry at fiesta with the newcomers. Estrada trusted that all would come out right. There was plenty of land for all. He had sixteen leagues, or over 70,000 acres, 12,000 cattle, and 4,000 horses. The mission storehouse of Santa Margarita at the head of the valley, where long ago priests in the wilderness had met to confess each other and had stored their corn against famine, was filled to the rafters with hay. Let some poor devil live on a bit of the land. They were good drinking companions and witty too and that paid their way. He didn't concern himself that they would *claim* the land.

But land troubles with squatters were only part of the difficulties now in the Salinas. Bands of horse thieves were constantly at work to make life miserable for rancheros. Things were in such a state that the new Americano governor McDougall had sent a military man, Selim Woodworth, with a company of men to hunt down the thieves and put on some "healthy hangings," in an effort to clear the valley of these marauders, but that didn't work, for the lawless ones knew by underground every movement of the military. It was well-known that there was a hangout of bandits at Espinosa's El Tucho grant near the mouth of the river, but there, because of rich soil, the mustard grew fifteen feet high and robbers were as elusive as fleas in the wool of a sheep. Woodworth and his men were eager to make a showing. They hanged some poor Mexicans and Indians who were innocent of crime, and the whole valley was up in arms against the military. If hanging was to be done it would be done by the people themselves when they were sure of the guilty one.

Finally a fighting British marine, named Henry Cocks, led a posse of six men to El Tucho. There they encountered the bandit Anastacio Garcia, who had run with the great desperado Joaquin Murietta, and was known as "Three-Fingered Jack." Garcia, a dead shot, barricaded his shack and managed to shoot two of the men.

British ire was aroused. "Fire the house!" Cocks roared. "We'll burn him out!" Runners went to a shack near by and got a can of coal oil. Bloodthirsty men climbed to the roof and poured oil over the flimsy weather-worn shakes. A match was touched!

Garcia, desperate now, opened the door, and from behind his wife's skirts potted another member of the posse. Bullets whizzed. Those who aimed tried to hit Garcia and miss the woman. Her arm was grazed and a bullet hit Garcia just below the shoulder as, sheltered by his wife, he made a dash for cover and was gone.

A Shrewd Man Arrives

M ARIANO MALARIN was having troubles of his own, managing the three great ranchos left to the family by the old Peruvian trader. Mariano's education for law in Peru was not much of a help when it came to the business of ranchos in the Salinas.

There was continual trouble with horse thieves and squatters, constant fees and lawyers to pay for the long-drawn-out process of confirming land titles. His sisters and mother had hearts too generous, and no idea of the value of money, and on top of that were brothers always in debt for fine horses and gambling chits.

Already Mariano had been forced to buy out Urbano's share of Guadalupe to settle gambling debts with Bidache, the French tumbler; and even Rafael Estrada, his cousin, married to Mariano's sister Isabel, had made his wife sign away her share of Guadalupe, and had spent the money. In order to hold the rancho together Mariano bought out Isabel's interest. Now, Estrada and Isabel were living on Rancho Rincon de las Salinas at the mouth of the river, where long ago Spaniards had taken out salt to ship to Mexico. Estrada was a canny one. Rancho Rincon de las Salinas was a fertile piece of 2,220 acres granted to a Spanish woman Cristina Delgado who had become infatuated with Rafael, who was full fifteen years younger than she was. She had given him her land and even paid for the confirmation of title. Rafael Estrada was living high now, with plenty of time to make fiesta and gamble while his wife Isabel added almost yearly to their family of puny babies.

Mariano struggled on, putting out a few hundred dollars here and a few hundred there. Money slipped away in driblets as easy and steadily as running water in the trough where fine-bred beef cattle of Rancho Guadalupe and Rancho Chualar went to drink.

Others who gambled in the Salinas and were short of cash gave their debtors a chunk of land, until now Espinosa's El Tucho alone had over half of it carved into small bits. Malarin land would not be carved up. It *must* be saved. Surely there was some way.

The "way" was David Jacks, a short squatty young Scotchman who wore a coat with a cape on it and was to play an enormous part in the future of the Salinas. He had come to California because he had read Walter Colton's articles telling of the golden opportunities. This canny Scot landed in San Francisco the year before Mariano Malarin's great need, with his sole savings of fourteen hundred dollars invested in pistols which had cost him eighteen dollars each.

San Francisco in 1849 was a wild town, where combination gambling houses and places of prostitution were the projects of French corporations which sent over crystal chandeliers to dazzle miners, and French mirrors where they could admire themselves, and French women to serve at roulette tables and relieve them of their money. In a town where single men gathered to spend their gold dust for drink, women, and gambling, there was a booming sale for firearms.

David Jacks disposed of his complete stock of pistols at fifty dollars each in forty-eight hours after he landed, and cleared four thousand dollars. Then he outfitted himself and started for the mines. But rains had washed out roads and bridges. Cabbage soup at two dollars a plate and soda biscuits at a dollar each soon took all appetite for the mines away from the Scot. Back he went to San Francisco, and then early in January he spent twenty-five dollars for a boat ticket to Monterey.

The four thousand dollars in the jeans of young David screamed for company. Cash was hard to come by in Monterey in 1850 and a good bargain could be made on most any street corner. A man who had pocket jingle was top dog. Say he loaned the four thousand on good security at two per cent a month, the parties agreeing to keep the loan two years and then to pay in full. *That* would be a good enough bargain. Twenty-four per cent a year for two years.

Mariano Malarin grabbed the hook. He put up the whole of old Juan Malarin's beloved Rancho Chualar as security and borrowed three thousand dollars, with agreement to keep the money two years at twenty-four per cent a year.

The Scot was a decent enough chap. He thought he was getting the best of the bargain, but Mariano knew better. He had high hopes for that three thousand dollars, and he would show a Scot how clever a Californian was in the matter of business.

A man with sharp eyes could see that Indian women with metates grinding corn was much too slow a process for these modern days when there were many people with mouths demanding meal. Any progressive man could sense the need for great grinding stones that would make meal faster and supply the demand of increased population. *That* man could coin money; that man would be Mariano Malarin. The whole Malarin family would have a share in the gains and even David Stewart Spence, son of Don David, the salter, who had married Marianos' sister Refugio, would gain.

The big stones for the mill arrived and with difficulty were set in place on old Juan's Buena Vista Rancho. But Mariano the dreamer had not reckoned with the boom at the mines. Laborers were in such demand in the Sierras that they could get a dollar an hour, and skilled mechanics demanded and received sixteen dollars a day. A mill required skilled men to run it. They had to be paid high to keep them from deserting for the mines. After corn was purchased and finally came from the mill, it had cost more than rancheros had to pay for corn and Indians to grind it. Labor troubles increased as the boom in the mines went higher. Mariano struggled hard against desperate odds with his mill, and borrowed more from Jacks on the Guadalupe Rancho to keep going. Then before even the title was confirmed by the United States Land Commission, David Jacks came to take the 8,889.68 acres of Rancho Chualar for his three thousand dollars and interest.

The Scot tried to make the situation as easy as he could. "I'll take the ranch, but when you get the money you can have it back," he told Mariano. "After all, I'm no rancher."

Never again could a generous-hearted Malarin tell a hard-up neighbor to "take a marquerna" of steers to eat from Rancho Chualar.

But there was trouble over Rancho Chualar, for Mariano had neglected to get the signatures of *all* his brothers and sisters who had an interest in the rancho. Refugio had not signed. The title was not clear. Jacks the Scotchman was soon to meet as a foe another canny Scot, Don David Spence.

Don David was related to Mariano Malarin in two ways, his wife Adelaida Estrada was sister to Mariano's mother, and his son David had married Mariano's sister Refugio, a cousin. Refugio had presented the old salter with a grandson the very first year of marriage.

Old Don David, who loved land, was not letting Chualar go out of the family as easily as Jacks expected. He went to his son David Stewart. "Jacks has his eye on Guadalupe next, for he has loaned Mariano money on the land. Don't let your wife Refugio sign a release of her interest in Chualar

Rancho until Jacks releases all hold on Guadalupe Rancho."
And so it was that a shrewd Scot outwitted another Scot and
saved Rancho Guadalupe for the children of the Spanish
soldier Estrada and the Peruvian trader Malarin.

The taste for land became an obsession with David
Jacks. He soon discovered that unbusinesslike Californians
in the Salinas were hard-pressed for money because of dry
years when they had been forced to sacrifice cattle, and they
were lax in the matter of taxes. The whole thing was simple.
The Scot began to pay delinquent taxes on good land without
troubling to notify the easygoing owners! Then when the
inevitable finale came, he shrugged his shoulders, pointed out
that he was within his legal rights, and if they would pay
him with interest they could have their land.

Piece after piece was added to his holdings through
mortgage and tax sales, and hatred burned in the eyes of
those who were turned off the land. So much hatred was gen-
erated that the shrewd Scotch landholder was compelled to
travel with a bodyguard, for several times angry Mexicans
and Californians took a pot shot at him.

During those hard years of the early fifties when land
was being confirmed or rejected by the United States Commission, many changes took place in the golden valley. The
old order gave way to the new.

Esteban Munras, the painter and grantee of the great
San Vicente Rancho, died before his title was confirmed and
left the San Vicente to his wife and children. Esteban of the
All-Seeing Eye was a foresighted Spaniard; he dreamed of
progress, and he had faith in his dreams. He was *sure* great
prosperity would come to the fertile valley after his bones
were interred in a cementario. He told his wife Catalina always
to hold on to her land, and one day there would be a town
on San Vicente where now cattle grazed in the golden fields.

"When the time is right, subdivide a portion of the
land of San Vicente into a township. Use the *poor* land, not

the fertile. *Give* one lot for a school, one for a church, and one for a cemetery, for surely one day a town will come."

Thus Esteban the artist planned for future folk from their childhood to their graves, and then left forever his beloved Salinas.

Changes had come also in the beautiful valley of the San Antonio River, and just five miles south of San Antonio Mission, where once padres had worked beside Indians in the fields and mission flocks had grazed in quiet, a settlement had started up. Jolon (valley of dead oaks), they called it. The place came into being because of gold miners. An inn was established for the new overland stage route plying between Los Angeles and San Francisco, and there was a little post office where letters with special stamps costing twenty cents and brought across the plains by pony express were left on the mantelpiece to be claimed by their owners. The Spaniard who kept the post office could neither read nor write.

Miners came into Jolon along grizzly-infested trails from the Santa Lucias to the west. Mexicans they were, and patient Chinese who could manage to pay the tax which gringos had levied against all "foreign" miners. At the "Last Chance" and the "Grizzly" they paid for drinks in gold dust.

Padre Doroteo Ambris, an Indian and the last wandering Franciscan priest left in the Salinas, shook his head over the change. He came as often as he could to San Antonio to keep track of the Indians round about, but there were so many poor Indians. They were now scattered through the dozens of secluded little valleys off the Salinas. These saloons at Jolon boded ill for Indian children and a padre could not always be there to watch out for them.

Not far away Ygnacio Pastor, the Indian, tilled the bit of land given him by the departing padres and sold vegetables, little knowing how much trouble and heartache was to come over his "Milpitas."

Bishop Alemany, fearful lest the unsold San Antonio

Mission should fall into greedy hands, asked that the church have title to the mission with a little land surrounding it.

Already there had been trouble with Mariano Soberanes over his greed for tiles from San Antonio. Brvt. Captain Henry W. Halleck, now Secretary of State under Governor Riley, had written to Soberanes from Monterey. The governor had given Mariano Soberanes permission to take tiles from the old uninhabitable buildings at the mission to tile a new building on his Los Ojitos Rancho not far away as compensation for Frémont's burning, but Soberanes had taken tiles from the perfect buildings. How the mad desire for possessions made men forget things sacred to a church! Soon there would be nothing left. The mission must be under church control. Surely the gringos would understand the feeling if they knew in Washington. Constantly the bishop sent pleas to the capital of "the States."

Once a month boats put in to a landing on the fierce rocky coast just over the range to bring food and supplies, which had to be landed by cable. Settlers around Jolon went by horseback over the dangerous trails. This boat bringing news from the outside world was the social event. Women as well as men made the hazardous trip, for there was calico to be had, and ribbons too. There was time for gossip and pickle recipes and patterns to be exchanged while they waited and listened for the boat's whistle. Feminine eyes eagerly scanned the stock of calicoes that brought a dollar a yard, and since there was only a bolt or two, each woman had to make her own dress different from the rest by cut or by handwork.

Many of the buildings of Our Lady of Solitude were now brown crumbling ruins since Alvarado had taken away the tiles that had protected adobe walls from melting away. Feliciano Soberanes had used some of the adobe bricks to restore a part of the church, and a sign told all who passed that this was the "Soledad Store." Travelers resting there were charged outrageously for crackers and cheese. Hospitality of padres in the wildereness was long forgotten.

Feliciano, comfortable in his big house in Monterey, had divided Soledad and sold his son Francisco four thousand acres for two thousand dollars. The land was measured by eye and missed by only fifty acres. Another son had 1,705 acres and a third, about the same amount. The next generation of Soberanes began to come into the world on the lands of Our Lady of Solitude.

After a marriage which had produced twenty-one children in twenty-five years, W. E. P. Hartnell, merchant, trader, schoolmaster, and translator of the constitution, was dead at fifty-six in his house at Monterey. In a beautifully penned will he bequeathed to his son Guillermo (William) his large family mourning ring, and to his other children keepsakes. To his brothers and sisters in England he willed money to be obtained at good exchange, and to his wife Teresa de la Guerra his mortgaged property. The will stated that any debtors to *him* were not to be distressed on account of the amounts they owed, but whatever they *chose* to pay was to be received in full of all demands.

Hartnell's widow had her troubles. A year after her husband's death the United States Land Commission confirmed to the estate only 2,971 acres of Alisal Rancho, instead of 6,660 acres that had been originally granted to the schoolmaster. The rest of Alisal, with the exception of what Alvarado held, was to be opened to homesteaders. Then came some dry years when cattle must be sacrificed, a wet year that spoiled the crops, and then the sale of a number of Hartnell's pieces of land. Among them was the Alisal, that place once so fraught with dreams and high hopes and learning. All this went for delinquent taxes to David Jacks the Scotchman for $122.

PART VIII

"Blue Bellied Black Republicans and Democratical Hypocritical Secessionists"

The Mysterious Stage Driver

THE NEW overland stages with their cumbersome square covered bodies slung on leather straps brought great excitement and a new era into the Salinas. These great rumbling vehicles with six lathering horses and a swearing driver, roared through the valley raising clouds of yellow dust and spreading a ribbon of news in their wake. They pulled together isolated ranchos that were twenty-five miles apart. Gossip about secession trouble in "the States" gleaned from Pony Express riders was passed on when the stage paused at scattered ranch houses to water horses. News of local births, scandals, and deaths traveled faster now, and sometimes the gleanings were even more exciting. The quicksands of the Salinas often shifted within a few hours and, without bridges, crossing the river was always a breath-taking and dangerous affair, or maybe the stage had turned over on the grade, or bandits had held it up.

Stage stops where travelers could eat a bite or lay their dusty, travel-dizzy heads of a night became necessary. Easygoing Salinas rancheros impoverished by the dry year, horse and cattle thieves, and land troubles, found a new way to pick up cash to tide them over.

Josefa Soberanes, daughter of Don Feliciano and grantee of Los Coches, was fortunate. Los Coches was at a crossroads which fed the old road to Soledad Mission and Paraíso Hot

Springs in the foothills, where long ago padres had soaked the weariness and aches from their bones. The big adobe house was also right on El Camino Real, the main stage road through the valley. Josefa had money troubles. The bill at Rodriquez's store for liquor and groceries that her Maryland husband Richardson bought was growing ever larger at two per cent a month and compound interest—nearly eighteen

LOS COCHES

hundred dollars. The stage brought money in hand from travelers, who welcomed the row of locust trees in front of Los Coches after the hot windy trip.

There were great doings too on the wide plain of the valley nearer the river's mouth. Deacon Elias Howe from Massachusetts, the adventurous son of the sewing machine inventor, had erected a two-story building in the mustard fields at the intersection where the road to Monterey met the Los Angeles road. He had an inn, post office and store, on the

King's Pasture where Spanish soldiers once had roped their own beef, and refugees had camped in 1818 when Bouchard the pirate and his Sandwich Islanders had burned and pillaged Monterey.

Valley rancheros tapped their heads in derision over this project of the whisky-bibbing Deacon Howe. An inn and a post office alone on the Salinas Plain so far from any settlement was utter foolhardiness. This "Boston man" was "poco loco" and didn't know the country. He was fair target for bandits and thieves and cutthroats. Besides, Natividad, a few miles to the east, was a real settlement of a hundred people. Stages would rather stop there. Did he think he could compete with an established settlement? Well, it was plain he would soon lose the inn and the few acres he had bought in a mustard field.

In spite of drought years and discouragement the New Englander went on planning and building, and offering drinks to those who tarried at his inn. Word traveled that Howe the gringo was a good judge of whisky. There was soon excitement enough at his crossroads, for the canny deacon put up bets on which stage would arrive first at his place—the Monterey-San Jose or the Los Angeles—and he backed a driver as a horseman would back a favorite horse; and, since the bets were paid in whisky, the drivers soon began to race across the plain to Howe's place. Whips cracked in an accompaniment to the swearing of drivers, stages lurched, and passengers shouted encouragement as the horses white with lather often arrived neck and neck at the innyard from different directions. Spanish and Mexican Californians, ever on the alert for anything that smacked of gambling, were soon drawn into the net and often put up money or even land on the stage arrivals. They rode their own horses to the inn, in order to be there first and have a few drinks with the deacon and to place their bets. Then there was celebration of the winner with rounds of drinks, when passengers and even hostlers were toasted. Business soon began to boom at Deacon Howe's crossroads in the mustard fields.

Then on October 24, 1861, the race was forgotten, for the stage from the north brought real news. The last wire of an overland telegraph had been put up. At San Francisco a noon telegram from New York had been received a few minutes after nine o'clock in the morning of the same day.

Gringos at Deacon Howe's went wild and treated everybody to drinks. They all wanted to send these quick messages at a dollar a word! But Californians knew better. How could these people turn *back* the clock from noon to nine the same day? It was just another Yankee smart trick, like claiming land that was not theirs, and stealing a ranchero's best horses while he was in his own bed at night making love to his own wife. But as long as these silly ones were wild with celebration and wanted to pay for the drinks, why not drink with them?

One of the favorite stagecoach drivers who came into Deacon Howe's tavern was Charley Parkhurst, a lean lantern-jawed tobacco-chewing chap in blue jeans who could cuss all other drivers clean off the road. Charley was fearless. If he saw a yellow cloud of dust in the valley, he lashed and cursed and roared the stage into motion, with no thought for the safety of his passengers, no thought at all but to beat hell out of that other stage and get to Howe's first! Whole cases of whisky were soon put up against Charley's prowess. Then suddenly Charley tired of it all and quit the road. He softened no end, and ran a little halfway house of his own for a while over near the coast. Not until after Charley died did those along the Salinas discover that "Charley Parkhurst" was a woman!

Mariano Malarin wished he could be so fortunate as to have a wayside inn where stage travelers would leave a little of their money, but no such luck.

Dry years had worked a great hardship on the Malarin estate. There was no longer a trunk under the bed where Mariano's brothers and sisters could go for money when they needed it. In order to keep the Guadalupe Rancho intact for the family, he had to borrow on Grandfather Estrada's beautiful Buena Vista from Cann Brothers, a firm of Jews who had a dry goods and mercantile business in Monterey. Now they demanded their money.

Mariano tried to put Cann Brothers off. After all he was courting Lola Pacheco whose father owned the San Felipe Rancho of seventeen thousand acres just over the mountain. It had once been part of Mission San Juan Bautista. Old Pacheco had a house of forty rooms and even a chapel, where he fed miners and put them up. He made the miners give a pinch of gold for a glass of milk, and he was very rich and generous too—a man who even settled handsomely on "catch colts," his children born out of wedlock. If only the Canns wouldn't *push*. If only Lola Pacheco would make up her mind.

But Lola didn't make up her mind in time, and the Canns were impatient to claim the 7,725 acres of beautiful Buena Vista Rancho which José Estrada the Spanish soldier had left to his daughter, who was Mariano's mother. Mariano got the signatures of his mother and brothers and sisters, and Buena Vista passed forever from Malarin hands.

The Jewish merchants took it for three thousand dollars. That fall Lola Pacheco married Mariano Malarin.

2

Gringo Fiestas

WAGON trains were now constantly on the move through Salinas Valley. "Blue Bellied Black Republicans" from Iowa, Michigan, Ohio and Illinois, and "Democratical Hypocritical Secessionists" from Missouri and Mississippi, who had gone first to Oregon and found the climate too wet, were now on their way to dry out in Texas. Many of them were just wandering worthless squatters seeking any way to live without too much work.

But the smiling fertile Salinas beckoned and held a substantial family of Democratical Hypocritical Secessionists from Mississippi. James Bardin, an ambitious man with a family, had seen the handwriting on the wall and had pulled out of Mississippi with his family and two of his black slaves and headed for Oregon by wagon train. Oregon with its soggy winters didn't appeal to Bardin the farmer, but mustard growing fifteen feet high in rich bottom land at the mouth of the Salinas was a different story. In no time at all James Bardin made a deal with Rafael Estrada who, now needing money at Rincon de las Salinas, was glad to sell 1,200 acres of the 2,220 given him by Cristina Delgado.

Estrada was pleased with the deal, for a man from Mississippi couldn't know that in wet years the treacherous Salinas swelled and swelled and changed its course until it washed away acres and acres of good bottom land, and after that the rancheros had only a willow thicket. Let the Democratical Secessionist find out for himself! The Bardins were proud of their new land. Not even the dry year discouraged them.

A little settlement had started a few miles away on El Tucho, which through continual mortgages and debts was gradually fading from the ownership of Espinosa. Bardin was pleased to have neighbors so near his wilderness of mustard. A man named White was there, and Henry Cocks, the fighting British marine who had cleared out Garcia the bandit. The settlement was known as Blanco, Spanish for White, after Thomas White. Each man had a few hundred acres that were productive, for now through drought, bad management, and clever gringo manipulation of squatter's land, the day of great ranchos was rapidly passing from the Salinas. In only a few years the average holding was pared from thousands of acres down to 466 acres.

Bardin added to his original land by buying claims from restless squatters who wanted to move on to new scenes. The Salinas would soon know that James Bardin and his sons had arrived. The Bardins someday would be among the few big landholders like J. B. Castro who had the great rancho across from the Estrada place where Bardin had bought land, or like Juan Bautista Cooper who had acres of land near the river's mouth, acres that extended into the sand dunes across the river. Yes, someday it would be the Bardins, and Castros, and Coopers at the mouth of the river.

The Mississippi Bardins were highly amused by Salinas threshing floors made of a circular five-foot wall of adobe forty to fifty feet in diameter where wild horses were turned in to trample grain and thresh it. Californians were behind the times, rather like people pictured in a Bible scene. The Bardins were likewise shocked at the bold way California women rode horses along with the men and used red satin sashes to tie them on the saddle. Mexican and Spanish women were like harlots smoking cigarettes in public! James Bardin's wife Lucinda enjoyed her pipe like a lady at her own fireside.

The Mississippi Democrats had brought their politics along with them to the Salinas, and soon found many other men of like mind. There were high and bitter arguments at crossroad taverns and stores when these Democrats met the Blue Bellied Black Republicans of California, who hated and feared all secessionists, for that meant insecurity in California.

Californians were sure these Democratical Hypocritical Secessionist strangers had come into California to take it over for the Southern Confederacy, and feeling was plenty hot. These people behind the Secessionist Democrat, Breckenridge, hoped to carry the California election.

Some easygoing Spanish Californians, more interested in making fiesta and naming new babies than in politics, shrugged their shoulders tolerantly and murmured the old Spanish saying about those who were enemies. "Well, we are not all gold pieces that everyone should love us!" Let the gringos fight over their elections. But Californians in the Salinas went to these new gringo fiestas called a political rally, where there was plenty of barbecued meat and vino, and the Secessionist devils paid for it. Listening to speeches made by gringos hour after hour was boring, but there were plenty of things to watch. Women had to nurse their babies, and lovers' eyes, filled with passion, were busy making trysts. The wine was good and the belly stretched tight with food. A few speeches didn't matter.

One gringo said: "If Lincoln's army is attacked as the food at these political rallies is, there will be nothing left of them. The Union is in danger!"

Another gringo looked over the crowd taking its ease under sycamores while an orator ranted, then shook his head. "No," said he, "they'll just get groggy with a bellyful of food and wine and the hungry Unionists'll catch 'em napping!"

3
Grizzly Adams

HOLY WEEK was early, but not early enough to catch spring flowers napping in the Salinas. During these few days that belonged to the Lord alone, all roads and trails led to San Antonio Mission. No pilgrims rode horseback save those too lame to make the trip on foot. Even the fine rich rancheros left their horses at least a mile away and proceeded afoot to San Antonio, in remembrance of the Man who walked a lonely path. Ragged Indians, stiff in the joints from many winters in the valley, trudged for miles through carpets of blue and gold, their eyes alight with memories of the days long gone, when padres had been at San Antonio to welcome them and give them corn. Magpies, used to having the valley to themselves, flicked black-and-white wings in resentment and kept up a constant chatter with their bright yellow bills.

Padre Doroteo Ambris had cleaned up the moldy old church. Wild flowers were everywhere and tapers burned brightly on the rickety altar. Beneath it lay the figure of the Blessed Lord lying in his sepulcher. Indian hands placed tight little bouquets of gaily colored posies at his feet in tribute. The old walls of San Antonio held close once more the soft-voiced chants that came from devout Indian throats and incense filled the air.

There was the "washing of feet," when fine dons forgot

their worldly possessions in humility of the Lord, and bathed brown horny feet of Indian servants. Little children in bright calico were wide-eyed and solemn while they watched. Two chosen ones in stiffly starched white robes were excitedly awaiting swan's wings to be pinned to their skinny shoulders, then they would be angels to stand guard at the altar.

The church was full. There was a beautiful Mass and all knelt on the rough floor while the padre who had come from a valley where he lived now among Indians, chanted a long list of saints. The Good God and the Blessed Mother and her Son and all the saints would know they were not forgotten by Indians, even though long ago Mexicans had sent the padres away from San Antonio. Perhaps if prayers were fervent enough it wouldn't matter that San Miguel was deserted and Our Lady of Solitude just a mound of adobe.

After the services, rancheros and Indians stood in little knots to exchange news of the Salinas Valley and its tributaries, while women kindled fires to heat up pots of frijoles. Wolves and grizzlies were worse all over. At Jolon Rancho, on the San Antonio River, a gringo from Virginia told that grizzlies had taken nearly all his calves! Bear hunters had been brought in, famous ones from the Valley of the Carmelo over near the coast, but still the grizzlies grew fat on yearlings. Bear stories soon vied with each other in ferocity and tonnage, as each man waited breathlessly to tell his troubles with the great beasts. One ranchero had seen with his own eyes a bear that weighed at least two tons!

It was then that a ranchero with land on the east side of the Salinas told a strange story.

One morning he had been out hunting a herd of wild cattle in a canyon that connected the Salinas with the San Joaquin, and he saw a man driving two mules hitched to a spring wagon. A great grizzly bear was trotting beside the wagon and a smaller bear with his feet tied up in rags sat

GRIZZLY ADAMS AND BEN FRANKLIN

atop the load, riding like a prince. While the ranchero watched unseen from the chaparral, the wagon capsized on the grade and went tumbling to the bottom. The man picked himself up and began talking to the bears. He talked to them as if they were people, and rubbed the bruised nose of one as a father would pacify a hurt child. He called the bears by name.

Eyebrows were lifted, heads tapped, and the ranchero was accused of drinking too much Yankee whisky. But he stuck to his story, and told how the man had mended a broken wheel and then pushed on to let his mules drink in a swampy place of the Salinas near San Miguel. The mules, eager for water, stood too long until quicksand began to take the wagon. It was then that the ranchero rode up and helped this queer heavily bearded man to pull out.

And a good deed it was too, a deed that brought many times its worth, for the man was James Capen Adams the hunter, with his tame bears Lady Washington and Ben Franklin. He had heard about the grizzlies in the Salinas and come to see them for himself. They had talked until late, and then "Grizzly" Adams and his bears and dog were invited to the rancho for dinner and to stay. The bears followed perfectly at heel.

What a visit they had. Grizzly told how he had given up women in favor of bears, because you could train them easier, and had trapped the cubs and taught them to help him catch other grizzlies.

They had fixed up the hurt mule, and then the ranchero told Adams of the trouble with bears and showed him the body of a calf killed only the night before, where it lay in the corral.

Instantly Grizzly had turned professional. He ordered all other cattle and calves out of the stockade, and when night came, all dogs were tied up and Spaniards were ordered to bed.

Grizzly concealed himself with the bear Ben Franklin and Rambler his dog, in a pile of logs near the corral and began his watch. It was moonlight. About ten o'clock the bear came, stepping boldly. He leaped over the side of the corral, which was five feet high, a great hulk of a creature. Grizzly let the bear eat, then crept to the side of the corral and placed his rifle over the edge, taking fair aim at the bear's shoulder. Then he fired! The bear fell. Adams called Ben the bear and Rambler his dog and they leaped into the enclosure and were soon upon the bear. They all rolled and scrambled together and kept the bear busy while Grizzly reloaded his rifle. Another shot. Still the bear was not killed.

By that time the noise was fierce. Everybody of the ranch came running with dogs. But Grizzly cursed loudly, ordered them all back, and turned again to the fight. The wounded brute now had Rambler in his jaws. He was shaking the very life out of the dog, while Ben the bear was doing his best to attract the wounded grizzly to himself. Adams jumped the fence, rushed up, and buried his knife in the brute's neck. He dropped the dog and turned on the man then. He tore the buckskin pants off him, but didn't do more, for faithful Ben worked hard and drew the bear's attention from his master by nipping. As the bleeding brute turned to Ben, Grizzly jabbed him several times with his knife behind the shoulder and in a few minutes rolled him over dead.

What a sight! The biggest bear they had ever seen, fine and fat on the best calves, now lay dead.

Such a fiesta! There had been toast after toast to the brave Americano and toasts for Ben and Lady Washington, and toasts to *luck,* for Grizzly was soon to exhibit them in San Francisco. Already a man named Barnum wanted them in New York.

After the story was finished rancheros wanted this man

James Capen Adams. He must come and rid them of *their* grizzlies! Where was he now? Send a rider!

But the ranchero shook his head. Adams had shot a few mustangs to eat in Pine Canyon, had put bear grease on Ben's feet to heal them where they had cracked as he walked over the dry sand, and then he had gone north to get ready for showing his pets in San Francisco.

James Capen Adams, who preferred bears to women, had come into the Salinas, done his brave deed, and wandered away again, but gratitude and the story of his bravery were to live on for generations.

4

Doings of an Italian Tinsmith

EXCITING news traveled through the valley by stage
and by hoof right along with the late spring rains. Alberto
Trescony, the once tattered Italian tinsmith of Monterey,
had for years been quietly buying up thousands of acres
in the Salinas just north of Mission San Miguel. In fact his
land still had adobe corrals where Mission San Antonio sheep
had once been penned at shearing time. Now, Trescony had
built an adobe house and was to live on his great rancho.
The very Estradas (cousins of Rafael at the river's mouth)
who had once owned the 8,874 acres of San Lucas grant that
Trescony had bought from a Britisher, could remember
when the Italian had arrived a few years before in Monterey,
ragged, with not even shoes to his feet. Why, Trescony the
tinsmith could neither read nor write, and now he had
twenty thousand acres of fine land in the valley! Not only
did he own San Lucas, Garcia's San Benito grant, but part
of the Soberanes' San Bernardo as well.

Garcias and others were open-mouthed over the doings
of the tinsmith, but soon wine flowed freely in an effort
to make them all forget the changing times along the river.
Then, because Spanish and Mexican Californians loved that
low form of biography called gossip even more than christenings or fiestas, tongues warmed by wine began to clack.
Trescony was soft-voiced and he never smiled, but it was

well-known that the tall stoop-shouldered Italian had made love to another man's wife in Monterey and married her before the sod had settled on her husband's grave!

Trescony was an orphan who had run away at twelve from his stepmother in northern Italy and gone to Paris to learn French and tinsmithing. He had told that much himself in Monterey to one of the Soberanes just after he arrived in 1842, when he begged for the old tin cans that were thrown out, and then made a little fire in the street to melt out and save the solder that held them together. And the clever tin cups he had made from those old cans and the solder that had been melted from them. The niños and niñas were wild for them; every ranchero's child living in Monterey must have one of the new cups made in the street by Trescony the tinsmith. He charged plenty, too, for what didn't cost him anything but a bit of time and some begging.

Estradas and Rodriquez, listening to the rain beat against the windows, remembered well the little shack Trescony had, all covered with bits of tin to make it proof from winter rains, and how on foggy nights when his house was cold the tinsmith sat alone at the end of a bar playing solitaire and soaking up the good warmth of the saloon. They had sent him plates of hot food, poor man, after guests had gone from wedding fiestas and christenings. He had always been so polite and grateful. Yes, and now he owned the fertile acres they had long ago lost to lawyers for land titles, or to gringos for fiesta money, or to tide them over hard years.

Trescony had knitted his own queer shoes. He said they were alpargatas like those worn in Italy; coarse wool tops, with braided straw soles sewed onto them. He knitted often as he walked in the streets, with long needles made from slender willow switches that he cut in the river bottom.

A Malarin remembered now how Trescony, usually a silent man, had once told that he came steerage from the

Old World to the New and then was shipped out to Texas in a car as animals were sent, to work on construction. He had learned that Mexico was paying a high bounty in order to get sheep into the country, and had saved his money penny by penny until he could buy three thousand sheep which took him a year to deliver on foot in Mexico City. That must have been when the Italian learned to speak Spanish like a native, for there was no book learning to him. He often admitted that he must carry everything in his memory since he could not figure or even read. And he had practiced for hours the signing of his name with fancy rubric tails to it.

More wine was passed, to wash down Spanish Californian throats the thoughts of Trescony's figuring! The gold rush up north, and Trescony in his little shack in Monterey making gold-washing cradles to be used in the mines. He sold them for thirty-five dollars each! Thousands of cradles he shipped out of Monterey by boat! That would take some headwork for a tinsmith who couldn't figure; a tinsmith who had walked from Mexico City to Mazatlán on the west coast to catch the American steamer for San Francisco.

The *Julia Liedsdorf* was the boat, named after the wife of the vice-consul under Thomas Larkin, and when she put into Monterey, the red-tiled roofs and white walls of the old Spanish capital had made Trescony homesick for Italy. He had stayed.

Yes, he had stayed to buy with his tin-cup and gold-cradle money the old Washington Hotel and remodel it in 1849, just seven years after he had landed. Trescony invited the whole town to fiesta that day and then rented the place for twelve hundred dollars a month to delegates who came to draw up the first constitution for California.

In his little tin shack, the tinsmith who couldn't figure was doing well, with fifty thousand dollars he had salted away. Next had come the great Tularcitos Rancho of forty thousand acres in the Carmelo, that Trescony bought from Ogletree. Some said he got it cheap, for bad debts.

Ogletree had been a smart one though, the gossipers remembered; he had in the agreement that Trescony was to continue the dairy, and keep on the thirty Chinese who were running the place. The tinsmith had vaqueros and milkers with queues, who packed butter in firkins to ship by boat from Monterey to the mines. Yong, the Chink teamster from Tularcitos, was as fine a teamster as ever drove eight horses to a plow. "And him not bigger than half an ordinary man and not even a whisker on his face!"

Among the gossipers there were bitter but admiring memories of Trescony's courage. Two men from old Spanish Salinas Valley families, now forced to work at roping for gringos, remembered how only a year or two ago there were too many stallions on Tularcitos and a lot of horses needed castrating. It was late in the season and the colts were old for the operation. There was danger of flies and infection, but Trescony insisted. "The horses will stand up to their bellies in the lake water and then roll in the mud. It will cake over the sore and they'll be all right," he told the ropers, who had only sniffed. Trescony the Italian didn't lose a horse.

The tinsmith had taken time for love too, everyone knew that. There had been the Irish Katherine Cotton married to the shipbuilder Rainey, and with two children. Well, the Soberanes, Estradas, and others just shrugged their shoulders over that. Some said they were lovers, others not, but after Rainey died, Trescony had married her. He had three children of his own now to leave his money to.

While the gossipers drank their wine and plowed up his past in dark furrows, the object of their talk, a weather-beaten man of forty-seven, with sharp black eyes, rode hunched up and weary through the sea of soggy yellow mustard that was part of his rancho in the Salinas.

Trescony was tired to the dropping point. Lambing season was on, and ewes were such silly creatures. He had worked day and night in the driving rain for a week, with only the Spaniard Marcos Garcia to help in the sheep fields, and brush shelters to protect new-born lambs from the harsh equinoctial storm. In Monterey his wife was none too well and he had no word from her. But thoughts of worry and weariness didn't leg a man on to success! Only cowards let fear creep into their bones along with the wet and cold to make them weak.

It was better to think of the yearlings he would have when skies were clear again. Great peaceful flocks of two thousand each grazing in the valley with their backs to the wind. And his house? It would soon be a good substantial affair of adobe bricks made by Indians, a house with plenty of rooms, fine and strong and true to the bob-and-line that he had set with his own hands. A place that would shelter proudly his children and their children's children, long after troubles with lambing in the rainy season had ceased to worry Alberto Trescony. Already the house was well on the way. Every morning he insisted, before he left, that Indians make a cross in the first brick to ensure blessing from the Good God who had given so much to the runaway orphan boy from Dromodossola in Italy.

He, Alberto Trescony, would fix everything so that his wife and children and *their* children down to the very end would have a good home and love and happiness and plenty, and never know the yearning that had eaten into the very core of his own heart. He had saved all but three lambs. What did it matter that the constant driving rain beat into the very bones of him, and that he was weary? A man dries out eventually, and he rests.

5

'She's Flooding!"

T HE RAIN kept up its ceaseless tattoo, day after day, week after week, that spring of 1862. Tons of water poured from side canyons and valleys, sweeping all before it into the Salinas. The roaring yellow river went over its banks and kept rising. Stagecoaches could no longer get through. Soon the Salinas went wild and ate away acres of land like a hungry wet devil that would never be satisfied! Fear glazed the eyes of "old ones" who had lived long in the valley.

Younger ones, seeing the cows and sheep they depended upon washed away, were working frantically in the pouring rain to save what they could.

Courageous rancheros clever with a riata fastened cables to trees on high ground; and then, holding to the anchored rope to keep from being washed away, they reached marooned animals which were then roped and tied and hauled to safety, feet up, across the roaring torrent. Lives were lost as well as houses and stock. And still rain came down in the Salinas, thirty inches of it. Trouble swept like a heartless brown monster from the head of the river to its great brown mouth.

At Santa Margarita Rancho, where padres had confessed each other and stored their corn, adobe ruins melted into soft brown mounds, but this no longer concerned the easygoing Don Joaquin Estrada. Two years ago he had finished up that rancho of seventy thousand acres for sprees to treat the gringos and had moved on to Atascadero Rancho. An Irishman, Murphy, had Santa Margarita and his vaqueros were working hard to get thousands of cattle to safety.

The fine new paper which President Abraham Lincoln had signed giving back to the church Mission San Antonio and Mission San Miguel and a bit of land on which they stood didn't help now. The All-Seeing Eye of long-gone Esteban Munras, looked down on six feet of water where Indian neophytes had knelt to pray, and water was flowing over floors in the cloisters that once had been stained by the blood of the braggart William Reed and his family.

Dark days of the heart, as well as rain and flood, had come to the brave and ambitious tinsmith Trescony, farther down the valley. Where once the mustard-bordered river bed had been narrow enough to call across in a normal voice, there was now a two-mile wide wash of sand, and Alberto's cheery Irish Katherine was in the cemetario, long past caring about rain and flood. Alberto had little children to think about and care for now, as well as his stock. The youngest boy Julius was only five years old.

Part of the great Rancho San Lorenzo farther down the river had long ago gone out of old Don Feliciano Soberanes' hands and been carved up because of mortgages. The best of it was now held by a San Francisco capitalist who had taken over. Gregory, the land lawyer, in consideration of five hundred dollars and the work he had done to confirm the title, owned many thousand acres which he had leased out.

Most of the buildingts were a melted brown heap at Our Lady of Solitude where Padre Sarria's cold hand had clung to the chalice even after the soul had left his starved body. The mission land that Don Feliciano had taken for a few mules and horses no longer concerned many members of the Soberanes family, for most of it had long ago gone for debts. Even the vineyard and the hot springs where padres had bathed were transferred to gringos who held out a mortgage to be redeemed. Seventeen hundred acres of what was left had been leased at a hundred and fifty dollars for two and a half years. Don Feliciano's son Francisco was living in Monterey. Most of the younger generation of Soberanes preferred living in town where there were more fiestas and cascarone balls, and something doing. They had left a mayordomo in charge of the ranchos, but times being what they were, many of the managers took too much for themselves. It was easier to rent and let someone else work.

Bishop Alemany and Padre Casanova of Monterey were sueing the Soberanes family for the church and a bit of land on which the one partly ruined building of Mission Soledad stood.

David Jacks, the shrewd Scotch moneylender of Monterey, seemed to prosper with the spring flood in the Salinas. His Chualar Rancho had suffered little. In fact a fine layer of valuable silt had been laid down where once there had been cobblestones.

He had rented five hundred acres of Chualar Rancho on shares to the hard-working Danish blacksmith James Iverson, who had come straight from Denmark to the Salinas and had saved up from his smithing enough to buy plow, horses, and seed. Iverson the Dane was to give Jacks half the crop and furnish everything but the land. The Scot was well-satisfied with his bargain. The Dane was tireless and full of ambition. With plow hitched and ready to go before dawn, and still at work as long as he could see at night, this man, used to the tight little fields of Denmark, saw opportunity in the wide spaces of the Salinas. But he plowed close to the fences just the same, and on a number of acres it meant the yield of an extra acre for Jacks as well as for himself. The Dane would show the easygoing Californians who had once owned the fertile lands of Chualar what could be done by ambition and hard work and in the meantime he, David Jacks could watch the money come in without making any effort himself.

Yes, things were going well for the Scotchman. He had heard recently that Rodriquez the storekeeper, who held an eighteen hundred dollar mortgage on the fine 8,794-acre Los Coches Rancho owned by Josefa Soberanes Richardson, wanted his money and already talked about a sheriff's sale to get it. Foreclosure on Los Coches was inevitable. Josefa was back on her interest and always wanting more money, and dry years and wet had taken most of the cattle. There was no use being sentimental about mortgages. Sentiment was a poor running mate for success in business. Could he, David Jacks, help it because Josefa and her husband ran up bills for goods they could not pay for? Luis Soberanes, Josefa's nephew, was now running the stage stop at Los Coches. It was called the Oak Grove House after the fine stand of great California oaks at the right of it, but from the tales that came along the valley, some of the money at the inn went for fiestas and cascarone balls that lasted all night and took plenty of purse jingle for food and drink. These Spaniards must have their fiestas even if the roof was going out from over them.

Jacks, the close-fisted Scotchman, married now a year to Christina Romie, the daughter of a German, had no patience with these cascarone affairs where men crushed eggshells filled with finely cut paper over the hair of the women they wished to dance with. It was said that some fool romantic Mexican or Spaniard even filled an eggshell with gold dust, so that it would glitter in the hair of the girl he loved, and she would think the more of him for it! Oh, well. Let them dance and dine and make fiesta as long as the money lasted. They didn't seem to mind plasters on their property, but there was bound to be a day of reckoning. He, David Jacks, could afford to wait. With the rich lands of Los Coches rented out on share as he had rented Chualar—well, that wouldn't be so bad. Los Coches added to what he already had would give him over forty thousand acres in the Salinas. Let these people along the valley give him black looks, or even threaten his life. He had power over them, because he had money. Now hatred of him was so great among the Mexicans and Spaniards that he was loath to eat in restaurants for fear of being poisoned. But a lunch from home in a bundle solved that problem. David Jacks with a bodyguard and a lunch was safe.

Young David Spence, living in the valley on the land the old Scotch salter had preserved intact, was worried some over the erosion of the river, but his house was high and safe and filled with happiness, for Refugio had just presented him with another son to keep young Rudolph and his little sister Helen Adelaida company. They would call this new baby born in a bad year, David, after his grandfather and his father.

In Monterey, old Don David was delighted. He had just received word that his claims to Llano de Buena Vista, which had been granted to the soldier Don José Estrada and left to Adelaida, and his own Encinal y Buena Esperanza Rancho were sure to be confirmed by the United States Land Commission. If the new grandson and his brother and sister followed the Scotch canniness of their grandfather Spence instead of the generous easygoing Malarins and Estradas, these 13,351 acres would keep them forever from knowing want. The Estradas might call him close and penny-pinching, but at least Don David Spence still had his original land and had saved Guadalupe for the Malarins! In spite of all the sound Scotch advice, Ignacio Malarin had sold out his share of Guadalupe to Mariano because Ignacio's wife had ambitions to be an actress and that took money. Urbano had already gambled away his share.

The flood had wiped out Ramona Malarin's new husband, the well-to-do Basque, José Somavia. He had lost fifteen thousand dollars' worth of cattle in Santa Barbara. But José Somavia was not downhearted. It took more than a flood to stop a courageous Basque bridegroom from making a living for his good and beautiful Ramona.

Ramona's brother, Mariano Malarin, and his wife Lola offered the Somavias the house they had built in Monterey, to live in until Somavia could do better. Mariano didn't worry much now about land in the Salinas, for in the background stood the ever-generous old Don Francisco Pacheco. Lola's father had even told Mariano to take money and make good the losses that had come to the Malarin family through Mariano's bad business judgment, but Mariano was a little too tight for that! What was gone was gone. It was better that Lola's inheritance should go to their own children, instead of to helping *his* brothers and sisters.

Water was up to the wainscoting in Deacon Howe's tavern at the crossroads, and there was little business now when horses and the stagecoach were unable to travel. The whisky-bibbing deacon tapped first one and then another of his stock of bottles and dreamed of Massachusetts.

Nearer the river's mouth, Castros, Cocks, Estradas, and Thomas White were camped on high ground and waited in the rain for the river to go down, so that they could see what was left of their land.

James Bardin, the Democratical Hypocritical Secessionist from Mississippi, began to think of higher land. No soil could stay with such a wild torrent washing over it. He took a deep breath, pulled in his belt and planned to operate a ferry across the Salinas where once it had been wide, but now would be a narrow channel. There were always people coming from the old capital at Monterey, on their way to Santa Cruz around the bay; they would like to get across. A ferry wouldn't be hard, a platform with ropes attached to each bank to pull on, and a pole to guide and push. Mississippi folk learned to accept reality and plan ahead.

Juan Bautista Castro, a descendant of the Castros who had come as colonists long ago with De Anza, was disgusted. What with wet years and dry, it didn't pay a man to ranch. He offered the thirty-six thousand acres of Rancho Bolsa Nueva y Moro Cojo, which he shared with his relatives Mrs. Merrit and Mrs. Sanchez, to anybody who would take it for eighteen thousand dollars; just fifty cents an acre, but no one came forward.

6

Salt Breast of Duck and Featherbeds
for Miners

O
N A BIT of low swampy salt-saturated land near
the river's mouth, Roleno de la Vierra, the Portuguese, and
his wife Polsena were in dire trouble. They owed thirty
dollars to Meyers the Jew. The flood had taken everything
but their shack, and there was a new baby on the way.
Roleno had worked hard at the mines for the little stake
they brought to the Salinas, and Polsena made it stretch as
far as she could. They had a good colt the first year, but
Indians stole it. Then crops withered before they matured,
and *now* the flood. The Jew wanted his money, long over-
due. There was only the cow.

"Give the cow to Meyers," Polsena told her husband,
and looked out the window at the pink sunset glow on the
flooded field where they had worked so hard together.

Roleno saw his baby at play on the floor, and his wife,
big with child, and shook his head. "Without the cow, we
cannot exist."

But Polsena insisted. What was right was right. You
contracted debts. They must be paid. The cow must go. The
Good God would make a way for them. Where was his faith?
Hadn't Russians long ago brought wild boars into California and loosed them, and hadn't the flood this day forced

one of the creatures right into their place? In the oven it was this minute, cooking too slow perhaps because the wood was wet, but food *had* come when they needed it.

Roleno reminded her of the stolen colt, the withered crops, the flood that had been visited on them. But not even this could shake Polsena's faith.

The next morning Roleno drove the cow before him over the hill toward the Jew's place. Polsena beat back the tears for a minute or two, then picked up her baby and strode through the soggy ground toward the beach. There would be shells to pick up, lovely fragile things with colors finer than a rainbow, and dainty white ones like milk. No *not* milk—marble. Don't think of milk now. Shells were everywhere on beaches, in California after a flood, and along the sunny shores of the Azores now so far away. God sent beautiful things like shells and laid them right at your feet for you to look at, and to help you as you prayed for the dark days to pass.

The high tide had washed up fish still struggling for breath, as it often did when spring rains made them numb from too much fresh water. Polsena picked up four or five of the shining beauties, and then paused to watch the Pacific Coast Steamship *Salinas* leave the landing established just a year before, the landing at the mouth of the Salinas where valley people hoped one day there would be a great city called St. Paul, after the town where an Americano who started the landing had come from. St. Paul landing was bound to succeed. Salinas Valley rancheros could bring here their goods for the mines so much more easily than going all the way over the mountains to Monterey.

Polsena sighed, and turned her eyes away from the sea. She tried to stop the yearning in her heart, that the *Salinas* might take something to the mines from the de la Vierras— something to bring in money for little clothes and to feed eager young mouths. Miners bought so much. They had hoped this year for a crop to send.

As she crossed the high white sand bar and waited a minute for breath while the child near her heart stirred restlessly, this woman from the Azores saw a great flock of wild ducks settle wearily on the soggy marsh. They, too, had their troubles in a storm. But *they* lived on and had their babies and came again to the marshes.

When night closed in and her daughter was tucked into bed, Polsena set a candle in the window and waited for Roleno. She had baked the fish as it was cooked in the Azores. Roleno would like the treat. Then in the dusk of the cabin while she waited, Polsena dreamed of fine things, as ever pioneer women on the frontier have dreamed first and then brought their dreams into reality by hard work.

But where was Roleno? Had he been caught in a new quicksand bed? This Salinas was treacherous. Fear had her, and she beat off its black wings by saying Hail Marys as fast as ever she could. After an hour went by, and the fish was past its delicious best, she wondered if he had forgotten time in the warmth of a saloon. Anger's claws pricked at her temper.

Then she heard footsteps. It didn't matter *where* Roleno had been. He was her man and he was home again! She listened. The slow slug of hooves pulling out of mud. An animal. From the open door she saw them come into the shaft of light, Roleno and the cow.

"Meyers didn't want the cow," Roleno explained as he took off his wet shoes. "He will stake us to seed if we will let him tell us when to sell our crop."

Polsena crossed herself and remembered another Jew.

Don Juan Bautista Castro of the next great rancho had not forgotten them. He came as soon as the water went down to learn how they fared. Seeing the pathetic field, he offered them a bit of his land, Mulligan's Hill he called it, with good soil to till. He would *give* it to them. Then Don Juan suddenly remembered that a sow of his had littered too soon because of the cold and flood and had died that afternoon. If Polsena would come and get the silly little squealers, she could have them for all of him.

Roleno jogged along behind on Castro's horse when he went home, lest the baby pigs die from cold and hunger in the night. Polsena, grateful once more to Meyers the Jew, heated cow's milk and began her toil of getting up in the night to feed the sucklings. But tiny pigs and a cow would bring in little in the way of money, and the land was too wet to move the shack—besides, the moving cost money, for men and horses were needed.

It was then that Polsena told her dreams to Roleno. They would salt the fish that came right to their feet on the beach. There was salt at hand, only kegs would be needed. They could ship kegs of salt fish from St. Paul landing to the mines and the de la Vierras would prosper. Ducks flew into their very dooryard; the Good God had sent them. Salt breast of duck would please miners who were hungry. If Roleno would get the ducks and the kegs she would do the rest. Miners needed feathers to keep them warm when icy winds blew over the Sierras. Duck feathers would warm miners and bring money to jingle in the pockets of Roleno and Polsena de la Vierra. All this had come as she waited in the dusk for a homing man.

The de la Vierras were never again to know want, but they knew backaches and weariness aplenty. From the start of a litter of sucklings Polsena later had five hundred pigs. She shipped kegs of salted pork as well as fish and breasts of duck and feather beds to the miners.

The faith and prayers of a woman from the Azores had been justified.

PART IX

Drought

The Little Matter of a Zero.
1863-1864

RANCHEROS and farmers in the Salinas had little time for thinking about the great upheaval over slavery in 1863, save to vote in a Republican over a Democrat by a majority of twenty thousand for the state. They were slaves themselves now, driven by the most cruel matser of all, drought!

For months and months now, no rain. On land that only last year had been underwater, crops withered before the very eyes. James Iverson, the Dane at Chualar, rubbed across his face a hand hardened from days on a plow, as if to shut out for even a minute the dry fields where spring barley had sprouted so eagerly and then died. His heart was sad, for his own letters in old-country script had gone home to Denmark about this great wide land in California where a hard-working man could soon find independence. He had told about his crop of sixty to seventy bushels of barley to the acre, and thousands of acres to be tilled. Those letters had brought his relatives and friends to the Salinas, away from Denmark where drought was unknown. The Jensens and Sorensens and Petersons had come with little else than willing hands and hopeful hearts to rent from Jacks and others on shares and till the barley land that now was laid waste by lack of rain. They had left a green country to come and push back the mustard of Salinas Valley and replace it with grain. He, James Iverson, had led his relatives and his friends into a land of drought. Now he would have to borrow, himself, for seed to plant next year.

On the few remaining big ranchos cattle were being sold off for a dollar and a half a head to save feed. Sheep bleated pitifully for food. There were plenty of bleats to fill the air that year of the great drought, for the fifteen hundred square miles of Salinas Plain contained more sheep than any other county in the United States—plus one hundred thousand cattle.

Frantic rancheros sold off great chunks of land, and put mortgages on everything they possessed in an effort to get hay enough to carry them through until rain came again. There were plenty of fights and much bloodshed between gringos and native Californians over pasture, for the valleys in the interior had dried first and cattlemen from San Joaquin drove weakened animals over the range in the hope that nearer the coast, where the fog was, pasturage would be better.

Kit Carson and his partner Joe Walker, Indian fighters and scouts, who had once traveled with Captain Frémont, but were now peaceable ranchers, drove their cattle over the hills from the San Joaquin into a fertile little valley that drained into the Salinas. Here they found feed nearly gone and the Indian priest Doroteo Ambris kneeling in prayer with his faithful Indians. They named the place Priest Valley, a name that never was changed. But Padre Doroteo and his Indians in prayer failed to bring rain. Not even the pitiful little celebration at San Antonio on St. Anthony's day helped.

People on their way to the celebration tried not to see the buzzards ranging overhead or smell the stench of carcasses or hear the pathetic bawling of cattle. It was said that one gringo rancher at Jolon could stand the frightful din no longer and had driven his animals over the ridge and down a chute into the sea.

Magpies sat in dried oaks with bills open. Only rattle-snakes thrived. Coyotes had no trouble of nights to eat, for cattle were too weak to run and grizzlies were numerous.

Mariano Soberanes let part of Los Ojitos go for feed, held high by a rancher who had a bit of flat land over near the coast where fog had kept the ground damp long enough to bring a crop of hay.

Trescony the tinsmith had no feed for his sheep, the same sheep he had fought to bring into the world in wet and rain while his Kate was sick; the sheep he had saved during the flood by driving them into hills where they were safe. When month after month of sun burned into the very clay of Rancho San Lucas, Trescony could stand the strain no longer. He sheared his animals and began to kill from sixty to a hundred a day, until three thousand were saved from the slow death of hunger and thirst. But the shrewd Italian tinsmith didn't leave his sheep where they fell, as many did that year in the Salinas. He skinned his sheep and rented the ruins of Soledad Mission in which to store the hides, and he hired an Indian to keep them turned so that worms would not injure them.

Hides would be scarce later when everybody had killed off sheep because of the drought. People all over "the States" would not stop wearing shoes because there had been no rain in California.

Garcia on the San Bernabe Rancho was crazed. He had fine cattle, bred for years to make a good herd, and now they were dying. Was he to just stand by and see the crea-tures go from under his very eyes? They were only bags of bones, his fine herd. A dozen times a day he raised a brown weather-beaten face to the sky. If only a cloud the size of a hand would come into that hard blue to encourage the soul of a man! If only a *sprinkle* would dull the frightful heat that made the temples beat with fear and worry. The nights held no rest from the terrible bawling. A whole twelve months without so much as a drop of moisture. God had forgotten his children and his animals.

In a corner of the adobe living room Garcia's wife Maria lighted tapers to the Blessed Mother and prayed.

Then one morning an Americano rode up to ask a drink of water. He was a new man about the valley and he told of rancheros farther down selling sheep for ten cents a head. But the Americano had faith in the valley. The drought would break.

"Aye," said Garcia. "If the ranchers aren't broken first. My cattle die before my very eyes!"

Then the Americano asked if Garcia would like to sell San Bernabe for five thousand dollars.

Garcia thought awhile. He looked out across the shimmering heat to where buzzards were attacking a fresh carcass, and he heard the last weak bawl from a steer that went down. If he sold San Bernabe for five thousand dollars and moved his cattle to another smaller rancho that he owned, why, then the money would buy feed enough to see the surviving animals through. Surely by that time there would be rain.

But five thousand dollars was so little for thousands of acres.

Out in the field a cow bawled helplessly.

"Yes," he said, "for five thousand cash." And he thought of those before him who had loved the San Bernabe when spring pricked through all green, and in the fall when golden rolling hills made a pleasant picture of contentment, as cattle walked slowly along the grooved side trails.

"Then I will attend to having the papers made out," the Americano said as he put spurs to his horse.

"And bring the money," Garcia called, "because I have

to send it before I can get feed from the north, from Oregon, to save my animals."

The man nodded, touched quirt to hat and was gone.

"You see?" Maria told him. "I prayed and the Americano came. The cattle will be saved!"

"But the San Bernabe," Garcia groaned. "The gringo takes the land of my fathers for only five thousand dollars."

"And what good is land if we lose the cattle?" Maria demanded. "Perhaps we have too much land."

The Americano brought papers; Garcia read them through quickly and then signed. He didn't want the very heart pulled out of him by lingering over the business. Then the Americano gave him five hundred dollars and Maria called them to eat.

As the Americano mounted his horse to leave, Garcia found tongue. "And when will you give me the rest, so I can be sure and save my cattle with feed money?" he asked.

"You get no more! That is all—five hundred dollars."

The man was crazed by the drought or Garcia's own ears perhaps deadened by so much bawling of cattle. Five hundred was but a drop of the money. It wouldn't last the cattle a week for feed! "What do you mean?" he asked. "It was five *thousand* cash for the San Bernabe."

The Americano only shrugged a blue-shirted shoulder. "Look what you signed, greaser." He held out the paper. A zero had been left off.

Another Spanish grant had changed hands in the Salinas for five hundred dollars.

Garcia could not fight without money. This was gringos' country now. He gambled his five hundred worth of feed against the drought and drought won! But there was a frightful stench from dead cattle to greet the new gringo owner of San Bernabe.

2

What Makes a Bandit?

FIVE MILES above San Antonio Mission in a big cave in the eastern wall of the San Antonio Valley, where once prehistoric men had worshiped, sat a grave, gray-eyed young man of twenty-four, a fugitive from justice and a hater of gringos. Tiburcio Vasquez, horse thief and bandit, had for the first time in his checkered career met an adversary he could not outwit—drought.

It was easy to stop a stagecoach, tie up and rob gringo passengers and leave them lying face up in the sun and then appropriate the fine sleek horses. It was even easier to steal a herd of gringo horses or a band of cattle at night. But now, higher up on the mountain in a hidden pasture stolen horses needed feed. Their helpless pleading eyes and dumb suffering cut into the heart of Vasquez as no human being could hurt him. How to get feed without paying the price of his own head in a noose? He had been out of San Quentin penitentiary less than a year for being caught red-handed in Los Angeles with stolen horses. It was not well to risk another bout with the law so soon. Gringo officers might not even take the trouble of trying him this time.

Vasquez looked around in the dim light at pictographs on the wall of the cave, men and animals and moons drawn by people who had lived in this wide valley of the Salinas before Indians or Spanish or Mexicans; people who had been free and happy with only grizzlies and wolves and wet and drought to fight; people who had never known the damned gringo and his greed and injustice! But for the gringos he, Tiburcio Vasquez, might even now be a decent Mexican citizen going on his way in peace. But what Mexican could live in peace now in California and still maintain his self-respect?

Vasquez looked back over the patches of light and dark in his life.

That first night in Monterey at the dance when it had come to him that a Mexican no longer had rights or even a chance in gringo-infested country.

He had been dancing at the fandango, in his best gold-embroidered clothes and a scarlet sash around his slim waist, with the prettiest señorita in the place. Ah, how her teeth gleamed and her eyes sparkled when he whispered flattery as they danced the jota. Then in came gringo men, pushing and shoving and snatching a girl from the very arms of a man, as the dance went on. Only seventeen he had been that night, when the gringos offered insult to California girls and monopolized the dance and the women. He had started a fight, a free-for-all with gringos. Someone shot out the lamps, and in the dark a gringo was knifed.

Three-Fingered Jack Garcia was at the dance and he had bragged how many gringos he had killed and how many Chink's eyes he had gouged out. Three-Fingered Jack was not in the hall when lamps were lighted again. But gringos wanted blood, and because he, Tiburcio Vasquez, had been seen with Garcia and had started the fight, they went after him. He ran away to the hill above Monterey and hid. Madre de Dios! That was the mistake; to run away made a man guilty in the eyes of gringos.

They had caught him and tried him in Monterey without any evidence, and then let him go, but from that night seven years ago, he was suspected—dogged. What chance had a Mexican Californian in a country where Americanos were officers and judges and controlled everything?

His father had given him cattle and he had tried ranching far away from Monterey, but always suspicion traveled by stage and by horse to follow him. There was no life, no freedom from prying Americano eyes. Did a man lose a horse or some cattle? Vasquez the greaser was hauled into court to tell where he was that night! Always a fight to prove innocence. After a while he decided he might as well be guilty.

He had gone home then to Monterey to eat tortillas and frijoles chinito (curly beans) with his mother and vow to get even with the Americanos. He had sworn to his mother on her prayerbook that he would murder no man. Then he went out and robbed gringo peddlers of their money in the Valley of the Salinas. Bigger things had inspired him after that. He could even smile now, as horses up in the pasture neighed for food, when he thought how he had stolen gringo cattle from over the hills and driven them to the camp of tattered half-starved Indians who had been cheated out of their land. That was a bright bit to remember! How their eyes shone like tapers on the altar at a nuptial Mass, when he called to them:

"Kill these steers, amigos, and eat gringo beef until the skin over your bellies is tight. When these are gone, Tiburcio Vasquez will get you more."

All Mexican and Spanish Californians as well as Indians had profited by the acts of Tiburcio Vasquez, and they paid well for beef and help. Many times they had hidden him from sharp-eyed gringo officers. Once he had been under the very skirts of an Indian woman when the sheriff and his posse rode into camp after him, and he had heard every word the gringos said. And another time he had crawled under the bedclothes of a California woman who had just given birth to a baby. At least a childbirth bed was sacred from sheriff's posses.

Sí! Why not remember the bright spots and forget the dark? The time that he, Vasquez the bandit, had cut a great band of sheep in two and given half to a struggling Mexican who had suffered at the hands of gringos. He had made life

TIBURCIO VASQUEZ—ROBIN HOOD OF
THE SALINAS

miserable for the greedy Americanos. Like a dog he was constantly nipping at their heels.

There had been days of love to remember too, with sweet-smelling wild flowers to lie upon and trees for a canopy, when he had quietly hidden out between robberies. Tiburcio never lacked for a woman to make love to. The women came to him and offered their charms! And why not? Tiburcio, the valorous, was young and slender and tender in the ways of passion. He had money for fine clothes and silver-trimmed saddles, and he brought them presents of shawls and gold earrings, and he didn't disappoint them in love-making as some worn-out husbands did.

He looked up at a red-painted animal on the wall; the red of quicksilver soil that had come from the east side of the Salinas Valley, where since time began quicksilver had been mined for Spain and Mexico. At the New Indria mine, among his friends who worked there, a woman had protected him once from officers and then left her husband for love of him, Tiburcio Vasquez. Because of that love a child wandered somewhere now without knowing a father.

No Vasquez gold had gone into wedding rings; he had seen to that! Three-Fingered Jack Garcia had joined him and his band along with other Mexicans and Spaniards who wanted to free California from the gringo, and they had robbed stagecoaches, so many that now he couldn't even count them. He, Vasquez, and his gang had taken five thousand dollars out of the wall at San Felipe Rancho, where old Francisco Pacheco had hidden it—Pacheco the Mexican who was too friendly with gringos and needed a lesson. It was true Pecheco charged gringos plenty for food and lodging, but nevertheless Pacheco thought too much about money and too little about the honor of Californians. When he was with the gang, Three-Fingered Jack was always worried about his wife. She was too pretty to be left so long without love and Three-Fingered Jack had swung by a noose at Monterey because his wife had talked too much. Gold in a wedding ring was a bad investment.

Up in the pasture above, a horse neighed pitifully for food and water, but the sun was too high and Indian scouts had not returned.

At last came a coyote call and an Indian slipped in beside Vasquez. He had located feed; a gringo over near the coast had hay left that had been cut from a high pasture.

The hay had been sold, but a dozen Indians could carry the whole lot on their backs in the dark of night. The dogs would not bark, for he, Rafael, had made friends with them as only Indians know how, while he talked to the gringo about work and looked over the place.

As dawn broke over the high hidden pasture, stolen Vasquez horses were quietly munching hay. Vasquez the bandit had outwitted both drought and a gringo ranchero.

3

Aftermath

WHEN Danes and Germans who tilled the bottom lands on shares for Jacks had lost everything and must begin all over again on borrowed money, and cattle had died by the thousands and sheep were all killed, the slave-driver drought loosed its hold on the Salinas. Softly one night rain came to the parched yellow earth, and men's souls once more expanded with hope and ambition. But for some the change had come too late, for hope was all they had left with which to gamble.

David Jacks, the moneylender, was a busy man, and the court a busy place when time turned over the page to 1865. Jacks began his work before mustard was yellow in the fields of Los Coches Rancho.

IN THE DISTRICT COURT OF THE THIRD JUDICIAL DISTRICT OF THE STATE OF CALIFORNIA, IN AND FOR THE COUNTY OF MONTEREY

Jacinto Rodriquez,
                    Plaintiff,
            vs.
William B. Richardson, Josefa
Soberanes de Richardson,
William R. Brown and David
Jacks,
                    Defendants

Action No. 465

Feb. 8, 1865. Action brought by plaintiff to obtain a decree for the foreclosure of a certain mortgage described in said complaint and executed by William B. Richardson and Josefa Soberanes de Richardson, his wife, on the 20th day of September, 1862, to secure the payment of a certain promissory note for the sum of $1800 in gold coin of the United States, dated the 20th day of September, 1862, with interest thereon at the rate of two per cent per month from date till paid; interest to compound every three months; that the premises conveyed by said mortgage may be sold, and the proceeds applied to the payment of said sum of money due on said note together with the interest thereon in gold coin of the U.S.

May 27, 1865. Sheriff's Return on Sale shows David Jacks highest bidder and the premises were struck off to him for the sum of $3,535.41.

The 8,794 acres of Los Coches was now the property of David Jacks, moneylender from Crieff in Scotland.

Luis Soberanes, Josefa's nephew, was to be allowed to stay on at Oak Grove Stage Stop, as renter on land that had belonged to his forefathers.

Don David Spence, that other wary old Scotch trader, fearful lest still another fickle season in the Salinas pile up his losses, leased 8,800 acres of tall fine-looking mustard fields to a newcomer, a Canadian who had lived in Vermont and come across the plains, a man who was to woo fortune, win her, and lose her in the Valley of the Salinas. Carlisle Abbott was his name, and he wanted to grow barley, seventy bushels to the acre, and run a dairy. He had brought five hundred cows from the north with him. Abbott had his eye on twelve thousand acres of San Lorenzo grant, which had been sold by Feliciano Soberanes for a mere token payment because of mortgages; but he leased the fertile acres of David Spence first for five years at five hundred dollars a year, and asked of the old salter the privilege of buying 4,440 acres of this ranch for fifteen thousand dollars. Carlisle Abbott liked the rich land of the Salinas, where wild oats grew well. This was a wide free land that got into the very veins after the hard scrabble on rocky New England farms. But grizzlies liked Abbott's dairy cows and bears were strong and bold after the months of drought, which had brought them plenty of food.

Spanish and Mexican Californians, forced into loss of land by the drought, went to work as vaqueros for this new man Abbott. They told the Canadian about bull-and-bear fights in the old days. They wanted a fiesta—a bull-and-bear fight! Sí, that would be fine; besides it would do away with at least one grizzly that ate cows.

Abbott was a wise man—a fiesta would make Spaniards happy and then they would work better.

Vaqueros went to work building a six-by-eight foot pen to catch the bear. They labored harder than ever they had toiled for Abbott, Wasn't this a fiesta? At last the trap was ready, a heavy wood stockade with a great door made from planks which they propped up and attached to a pole in the enclosure, where they tied a young calf. As soon as night came, a huge bear marched into the trap, the door closed behind him and he was a prisoner!

All along the Salinas word went out about the bull-and-bear fight on Sunday after Mass! Notices were tacked on posts and trees at crossroads. Fiesta! Fiesta!

Soberanes, Castros, Espinosas, Malarins, Estradas, and Garcias all forgot flood and drought and sorrow. A bull-and-bear fight. Hundreds of people came to the rancho by the river, where a great bull, with horns filed until they were sharp as a bandit's knife, waited for the proper time to fight the grizzly.

When everything was in readiness, excited vaqueros, dressed in their best, lassoed and threw the bull and tied one of his front feet to the end of a long chain. Then the bear was let out of his cage, lassoed and thrown, and the other end of the chain fastened to one of his front feet. This was to prevent either from running away from the other, and to ensure a fight. Both animals were now loose in a big corral.

Music started. A Mexican, astride a pinto horse old as its rider, sawed out a lively tune on a cracked fiddle. Bets were made two to one in favor of the bear as the fight started!

On the hay of the barn sat women in their finery, nursing babies, and crying "Bravo, toro!" when the bull had the best of it, and "Bravo, oso!" when the bear got his arms around the bull's neck. Crowded about the fences were men. Children darted about the place like bright colored flies, as they ate toasted salted pumpkin seeds.

The bear squeezed slowly with great arms until veins stood out on the neck of the bull! Bets went higher for the bear as he took a toothhold. And then Old Toro, by a mighty effort, got one of his sharpened horns between the bear's ribs, tossed him three feet into the air, and the fight ended! Old grizzly died a few minutes later.

Madre de Dios, what a fiesta! Vino! Enchiladas! Memories of olden days before the gringo, before tax troubles, and confirmation of titles! The mummified Mexican hacking away on his cracked fiddle watched coins fall fast around him, coins that sweetened the winnings on a Sunday after Mass. What did it matter that land was gone, that horses and cattle had died? Drink to toro and remember this day!

4

"Abe Lincoln's Been Shot!"

T HERE WAS a bounteous crop along the Salinas that
year of 1865 after the drought, as though the valley would
try to make up for the sorrow and loss of those who had
struggled so hard.

Trescony, the Italian tinsmith, did well with his stored
hides at Mission Soledad, for prices were high now when
sheep were scarce. He sold the hides for more than he would
have made if he had kept his sheep and fed them in a normal
year. He had money now to invest, and had one eye on
Deacon Howe's tavern in the mustard field. Dry years and
wet years had turned the deacon's mind homeward to the
built-up country of New England, where long ago men had
forgotten the troubled frontier. The winters there were hard,
it was true, but whisky was cheaper in Massachusetts, and
whisky warmed the cockles of a man's heart. Trescony could
have the tavern and all the land around it for eight hundred
dollars. It was a going concern, Deacon Howe reminded
Trescony—which way it was going he failed to mention.
The tinsmith took time to think.

At the landing on the river's mouth things were hum-
ming. Wagons piled high with produce were often backed
up five miles from the landing just waiting for boats! This
was the only way goods could be transported except through
Monterey or over uneven roads with spring wagons to San
Francisco. That took a week's travel and didn't pay.

There was another man at the "landing" now, and no city of St. Paul. The dreamer whose hope that had been was long gone. This new man, Charlie Moss, was a New Englander, a staunch Republican, a hater of Secessionists, who had come to California and married a woman from Chile. He was ambitious, was Charlie Moss, and he ran barges up the slough almost to where Deacon Howe's tavern stood in the mustard fields at the crossroads. He also had warehouses to rent. But Charlie Moss took his politics seriously, and there at the mouth of the river among Secessionists, war spirit ran so high that men even went gunning for each other over their politics. Charlie Moss was among political foes.

One warm morning in April as Charlie Moss worked at loading a boat, word came by rider that Abraham Lincoln had been assassinated! Moss stood for a moment and thought of the brave man lying dead in Washington. A boat must go out, even though a hero was dead, for living people at mines depended upon produce from the Salinas. Then Charlie Moss turned to his two young sons, William, thirteen, and James, eleven. "Lincoln's been killed by a damned Southerner!" he said between set jaws. "Go home, you two, and place the flag on our home hill at half-mast, and guard it well in memory of a great man."

The house was a mile away surrounded by a tall picket fence, and little Jimmie was frightened, for he had heard loud talk and seen the black looks over politics. He hung back. But Charlie Moss was firm, and brother William didn't know the meaning of fear. They started out together for home.

First, William went into the house and loaded up the double-barreled shotgun with twenty-one buckshot in each barrel. Then two pairs of grubby little hands pulled the flag to half-mast and the boys took up station in front of the house to await developments.

There was not long to wait, for a Secessionist on the

wharf had listened to Charlie Moss's orders, and news of politics traveled fast. On a rise overlooking the house there appeared half a dozen Secessionists who had heard the news and were now half-drunk on their way to a meeting to celebrate the killing of that tyrant Lincoln! They jeered at little William and Jimmie; they cursed Lincoln and his armies that went to fight for niggers. Then, when nothing happened, they put spurs to horses and galloped up the lane to the house and ordered the boys to take down the flag or they would come over the fence and cut it down!

"It stays," roared young William. "My father told us to put it up. I'll shoot the first man that tries to climb the halyards!"

The Southerners jumped from their horses and made a rush as if to scale the fence, and overpower the boy.

"Get out of the way," William told little Jimmie. Then he put the gun to his shoulder, so that the intruders were looking into its very muzzle. "I'll shoot!" he roared, "if you so much as move a muscle."

For a minute no one stirred. Jimmie covered his ears and looked away.

The Secessionists turned and walked to their horses. They cursed and jeered the "black Republicans" and threatened the boys at every step. But at Moss Landing on the mouth of the Salinas, so far away from Washington, Old Glory waved at half-mast until sunset, guarded by a little lad in a faded red jersey!

As skies darkened for rain in December of that year, David Jacks was busy once more, this time about the land of Alisal which the United States government had failed to confirm in Hartnell's piece, and had opened for homesteaders. The following recorded document stands ever as a reminder of two struggling ranchers who tried to beat drought and debt in the race for existence and went down to defeat.

Know all men by these presents that we, Manuel Maturana and Maria Teresa Maturana, his wife, of the County of Monterey, State of California, for and in consideration of One Dollar to him in hand paid by D. Jacks, the receipt of which is hereby acknowledged, have released, abandoned and given up all right of homestead in the Rancho of Alisal in said County and by these presents does release, abandon and forever give up all right of homestead in said rancho known as and called Alisal, also sometimes called the Rancho of Patrocino, on which they now reside.

In witness whereof we have hereto set our hands and seals at Monterey the 4th day of December, 1865.

Mª Teresa de Maturana   (Seal)

Manuel Maturana   (Seal)

State of California, County of Monterey. ss.

On this 4th day of December, A.D. 1865, before me, John D. Callaghan, a notary public in and for Monterey County, duly commissioned and sworn, personally appeared Manuel Maturana and his wife Mª Teresa de Maturana, personally known to me to be the individuals described in and who executed the annexed instruments as parties thereto and acknowledged to me that they executed the same freely and voluntarily and for the uses and purposes therein mentioned. And the said Mª Teresa de Maturana, wife of said Manuel Maturana, having been by me first acquainted with the contents of said instrument acknowledged to me on examination apart from and without the hearing of her husband that she executed the same freely and voluntarily without fear or compulsion or undue influence of her husband and that she does not wish to retract the execution of the same.

In witness whereof I have hereunto set my hand and affixed my official seal the day and year first above mentioned.

J. D. Callaghan   Notary Public   (Seal)

When Christmas came that year of 1865, Doroteo Ambris, the Indian priest, gathered his little band of worshipers for midnight Mass at San Antonio Mission, where once over twelve hundred neophytes had knelt to let the Good God know the birthday of his Only Son was not forgotten. The roof leaked as they moved toward the rickety altar with tapers that would guide the Blessed Lord over the wild hills of Salinas Valley to the first mission which padres had built so long ago in the region. But the saints, placed on their shelves by padres, were still there in spite of the cracked wall, and sweetness of Indian voices made up for the lack of volume when they sang to celebrate the birthday of the Blessed Babe. There would be no fiesta tomorrow as there used to be; but when they left, the padre gave each worshiper a little bag of corn and beans that he had begged from rich rancheros, and told them to remember grace before they ate on Christ's birthday.

PART X

Deer, Antelope and Close Votes. 1872

A Jew Goes Woolgathering

POLITICS along the Salinas boiled as actively as ever grapes had worked in wine vats of the padres. There were very few voters in the valley, so few that one vote could turn an election in the County of Monterey.

Secessionist Democrats worked against native Californians who were openly called "black Republicans," because they were on the same side as the black men of the South, and against slavery. It was no rare occurrence for a man born Mexican or Spanish, who had settled along the Salinas before American occupation, to be called a "damned Yankee" because of his politics. And Mexicans converted by Democrats were called "copperheads"!

Under this seething and boiling there was greed, ever the bedfellow of politics. And things were soon to happen in the Salinas, great things which would herald even greater things to come. The news of impending events was brought to the valley by a Jew, who was to spread his message, have the wits frightened out of him, and return no more.

He drove two mules hitched to a spring wagon, and he bought wool from rancheros. He told that in San Francisco three rich men, who had made money in the mines—Collis Huntington, Leland Stanford, and Mark Hopkins—planned to build a railroad into the Salinas to carry produce and to compete with boats in the haul to San Francisco. They had raised the money and already talked about the crews of Chinese coolies who were on the way from China to make roadbed and lay rails for fifty cents a day and rice. There was great excitement in San Francisco about this. Men were making speeches in vacant lots, because Chinamen were coming to work and cheat the white Californians out of jobs. White men couldn't live on fifty cents a day; white men hated the sight of rice! These rich men who were to run rails into the Salinas would grow richer on the sweat of Chinks.

The Jew went on his way, gleaning wool that sheep had left on fences. At each rancho he bought a little wool and told his story, until dusk fell, when he stopped for the night under a great oak on the San Lorenzo Rancho. Here, on land that Soberanes had grabbed from Mexicans and lost to the gringos, he gathered dried stalks of mustard to make his bed.

While the woolgatherer cut mustard stalks and piled them high for his bed, a great she-grizzly had the same idea, in about the same place. They worked back to back in the bedmaking process, each intent on his own comfort and oblivious of the other until the man cut a last armful and the grizzly saw him through the thinned-out brush. She stampeded the mules and overturned the wagon; then she treed the woolgathering merchant and kept him there until daylight! The next day this messenger of progress came down, picked up his wool, hunted his mules and drove forever out of the Salinas.

But the message had its effect from the mouth of the river to its head. An election was imminent, and now when the railroad was coming many men saw the need for political power.

Juan Bautista Castro at the river's mouth had tried in vain to sell his land for fifty cents an acre and failed. He had subdivided some of it to form a town. But not even that had helped. Now, with the railroad coming, he proposed to *make* the town take shape and sell lots. The place would be called

Castroville, Castro's town. Time was valuable, and not a minute must be wasted if he would win out over the gringos who had bought Deacon Howe's tavern from Trescony the tinsmith. They had sold the inn to Abbott the Canadian and it was now the Abbott House. These men, Riker, Jackson, and Sherwood, had already laid out a town in the mustard fields around the Abbott House, and they called it Salinas City. They were working now on rancheros of the valley to have the courthouse moved from Monterey, where it had always been, into the mustard fields where Deacon Howe had settled. It was to be on the ballot for all to decide at this voting. He, Juan Bautista Castro, whose ancestors had come with De Anza as colonists, was not going to let gringos get ahead of him. Castroville would be the great city in the Valley of the Salinas, not this wilderness town in the mustard fields that gringos called Salinas City.

J. B. Castro worked fast to bring people to start a town. He gave lots to the poor who needed them and there were plenty to accept! They piled their belongings into wagons and came there to settle. The railroad people would see. Castroville would be a going town while gringos laying out Salinas City were still getting lost in the mustard fields farther up the valley. Castroville would be established and ready to welcome the railroad.

But people without homes didn't make a city. He, J. B. Castro, would run for county supervisor for the district, so that he would have the power to get county help for his poor and they could build houses in his town of Castroville. But Castro had to fight the Secessionists, the southern-minded gringos, and he knew he could never get enough votes there at the mouth of the river.

Just as his uncle, the general, twenty years before had used strategy to win battles with wits instead of bloodshed, J. B. Castro used strategy now. He went over to the oldest huddled little settlement of Sotoville in the Salinas, where

Indians and paisanos struggled for existence; and he moved them, tortilla pans and all, and established them in Juan Pombert's little wooden hotel on his rancho for ninety days. Then he registered them ready for the voting! Some could not write, nor read a ballot in English, but he, J. B. Castro, would make the ballots for them to copy.

Juan Pombert, the son of a French-Canadian trapper who had come into the Salinas with Jedediah Smith, was to have his reward, too, for putting up these tattered ones in his little inn. If Castro was elected, Juan Pombert was to be roadmaster of the district.

2

Election Returns!

CARLISLE ABBOTT on Spence's land also was busy with politics. He wanted to be a delegate to the National Republican Convention, and to become a member of the California Assembly. He was a big landholder now, with 12,000 acres of San Lorenzo Rancho, beside the 4,400 acres he had bought from Spence.

Don David Spence the salter and trader was sad now, and thankful to let some of his land go, for just two years earlier that terrible thing called diphtheria had taken his only son and two grandchildren all in one month. At seventy-three, the old man was weary, and responsibility for the land must rest on the shoulders of his grandson, young David Stewart Spence. This new man Abbott was ambitious. Whatever helped him would help the Spences. Already Abbott was talking of building a narrow-gauge railroad from the fields of Salinas Valley to the port of Monterey, and this would help the Salinas Valley rancheros move their produce faster.

Abbott worked hard on his politics, as hard as he did on his ranchos, for each would help the other. He made friends with Democrats and Republicans alike, for personality counted with these Spaniards and Mexicans more than party politics if things were worked right.

To the south at the little settlement and stage stop of Jolon there was a Mexican in power, a Democrat, who could

197

influence all the votes there; but Abbott was a Republican. Without those votes he could not get in. Someone who knew them must guide their heads and hands in the matter of a cross in the proper place.

Abbott got Jacob Leese, a Californian married into the Vallejo family, to go to the Mexican. Leese promised that Abbott if elected would free the Mexican's brother from prison where he was incarcerated for stealing a horse.

At a stagecoach stop near the head of the valley politics were hot. An old man sat on the windowsill talking about the election; his oratory grew so heated that he had to use both hands; he lost balance, fell out of the window, knocked his head on the road and was silenced! There was a great to-do. Candidates and their representatives from both sides fussed over him. A Democrat even called the midwife to nurse him, not for his health, but for his vote. After several days of nursing at Democratic expense, and with election day too close for comfort, the old Spaniard opened one eye.

"Don't worry," he cried in as strong a voice as he could muster. "I'll be able to vote. No damned Democrat will win in the Salinas, even if I have to come back from hell to vote Republican!"

Carlisle Abbott won by a majority of six votes, and later managed to get appointed on the State Prison Committee. The horse thief was freed.

J. B. Castro also won the election as supervisor for his district. Hadn't he given free land to the poor? You couldn't take a man's land and vote against him no matter what party you said you were. Besides, he promised wooden shacks for all who voted for him.

Wooden shacks built with county money soon began to appear in Don Juan Castro's fields. Castroville was on its way! But Salinas City had the courthouse by nine hundred votes.

The Salinas Valley was coming into its own. David

Jacks was busy too. Since towns were all the fashion now, he was laying out a town of his own at Chualar Rancho that he had taken from the Malarins for three thousand dollars. A town at Chualar Rancho would increase the value of land. Pigweed was not a good name in English for a town but Chualar sounded soft and pleasant to the ear, and soon Spaniards would be so few that the meaning would be lost. The Danes who tilled the land would not care about the name so long as a town was there to help them.

Meanwhile patient Chinese laborers pushed on day by day, foot by foot, loading dirt, setting ties, and laying the bright steel that was to change forever the wilderness of the Salinas. On they went, over the salt marshes where the first Spaniards had taken out salt to be shipped to Mexico, and where not too long before the Portuguese Roleno and Polsena de la Vierra had watched the purple glow of sunset on their flooded fields. On and on went the rails.

At Castroville, the railroad men talked to J. B. Castro. A roundhouse would be good there, a place to keep engines and where crews could be established to take care of the trains. They offered Don Juan a price for a piece of his land.

"No! No!" he roared. "Madre de Dios! That is not enough for the land of my fathers. Would you cheat my children and grandchildren out of their land like common robbers?" Then he told them *his* price for the land.

On and on pushed the sweating Chinese, drinking dippers full of water from shiny tin pails, so that they would have sweat to pour out on roadbed and rail. On went the railroad past Castroville! Railroad men would not cheat Castro's grandchildren. The rails pushed on into the mustard fields where Deacon Howe's tavern stood in the center of a place called Salinas City. The gringos Sherwood, Riker and Jackson would *give* the railroad land for a roundhouse, and land for extra switch tracks. The railroad accepted.

One wet afternoon near the end of September, 1872, rancheros and farmers rode in from all directions and stood in the wind and rain to watch the last spike driven at Salinas City. There was a salute of a hundred guns and the first train, freight with thirty cars behind it, came into the new frame depot.

Up the line, Castro's town was merely a twenty-minute eating stop. Railroad men had ignored Don Juan.

Jacks, the moneylender, was a shrewder man. Painlessly he pulled strings in San Francisco, and by December of that same year gray steel pushed still farther along the valley to his Chualar in the wilderness, for there was business, barley to be shipped that Danes grew on shares.

Herds of deer and antelope grazing were startled by the sound of spikes hammered against steel and wood by sweating yellow Celestials pleased to earn fifty cents a day and rice.

ANTELOPE

3

Hangman's Noose on a Friend. 1875

SURVEYORS were busy in fields of the great San
Vicente Rancho, where Esteban Munras had dreamed of a
town. The widow of that painter of the All-Seeing Eye at
San Miguel and her children had decided that the time had
come to make old Esteban's dream a reality. "On poor land
no good for tilling, a town to help all rancheros around.
One lot for a school, one for a church, and one for a cemetario where God would give rest to his workers." Already
the rails were creeping like silver ribbons toward Rancho San
Vicente. Should the town be called Munras after the devout
one who had served so lovingly at San Miguel? No! No!
Old Esteban would not want that. Not far away was the
brown mound where once had stood Mission Soledad, forgotten now by all but the very old. The town must be called
Soledad in memory of the padres who had braved the wilderness of Salinas, to bring land and blessings to the children
and grandchildren of Esteban Munras. "Soledad" should be
printed on railroad maps, for future ones, so they would
know there had once been a mission dedicated to Our Lady
of Solitude, where Indians and padres had labored for God
in the fertile Salinas.

As surveyors called out their readings across the fields
of San Vicente, making ready for a town, another call echoed
along the valley.

"Vasquez the bandit is hanged at San Jose! Vasquez was betrayed by a woman who had been his mistress, who had slept in his very arms. She had fed him and trapped him while he ate. The crafty gringo officers had hidden under logs of a load of wood in a wagon and driven up under the very nose of Vasquez. There had been no escape, for they shot at him when he dived through a window. Aye, the valorous one had been brave then. He saluted them and smiled at their victory!"

Vasquez had been tried by gringos in San Jose; Vasquez friend to Indian, Mexican, and Spaniard was hanged. He was *dead!*

Lips that had met his in impassioned kisses quivered, and hearts contracted in sorrow along the Salinas. Many a taper was burned surreptitiously at small rancho altars, for the soul of a gay caballero with a gold-embroidered jacket.

In the hills, Indian stomachs would never again be stretched tight over gringo beef that was a gift from the bandit they all loved.

Vasquez was dead. A woman had deceived him—for a price! There was no one left now to fight for Indians, Mexicans, and Spaniards against the gringos. Vasquez, their friend, was hanged by a rope!

Indians were having a hard time now with the new order. If they came down from their mountain fastnesses, too wild for gringos, because drought had taken their corn and didn't find work right away they were called a new and terrible name, "vagrant," which meant jail even if all they had done was to sit in the sun along roads. They didn't understand or know what to do about this new thing, or how to avoid trouble with the white men. The jail was always full until David Jacks, the landed Scotchman, thought of a way.

The county couldn't take care of all these "vagrants." There was no place left in the jail and it took a lot of money to feed them. David Jacks went to the hard-pressed, penny-pinching county officials. He would take the Indians off their hands and feed them at no expense to the county. He would be responsible for them. They could work on his land, harvest potatoes on the four hundred acres of El Tucho that was left of Espinosa's grant, which had just been confirmed to him by the government.

Eureka! The solution. David Jacks the Scotchman worked vagrants under the hot sun for their food in this first slave-free state of California.

4

Railroad with a Chaplain

BUT DAVID JACKS was a good man in his way. He was a presiding elder of the Methodist Church Conference in San Francisco that year, and already had given land, acres of it, on the seaside near Monterey for a camp-meeting ground called Pacific Grove Retreat, where yearly revivals could be conducted by good speakers for the uplift and help of churchfolks. And Jacks no Methodist at all, but a good sound Scotch Presbyterian. He had even given money to build a Presbyterian church in Monterey. Yes, he was good in his way. In dry years he had distributed food to all the needy of Monterey, and his wife Christina always was handing out baskets from the back door. Jacks simply did not confuse good business with charity. Easygoing Californians didn't seem to understand about business; they were all mixed up about these things belonging together. Indians and churches had nothing in common!

Jacks was a foresighted man, who, even as the Indians worked on his land, had raised twenty-five thousand dollars on the Chualar Rancho which he had taken for a three thousand dollar mortgage. He had gone in with Carlisle Abbott, the Canadian, to build a narrow-gauge railroad to connect Monterey, twenty miles away, with the Salinas Valley, and reduce freight rates for rancheros. Cheaper freight would come, with the narrow-gauge taking produce to the boats at

Monterey. The new Southern Pacific wouldn't go to Monterey; they had no relish for bridging the ever-changing river bed of the Salinas. The name of David Jacks would go down as doing his part to open up the country and save it from the manna ways of easygoing Mexicans and Californians. Let the country grow, and grow with it, that was progress. Then all would prosper.

Jacks already owned most of the public lands of the Pueblo of Monterey given to the town by the Spanish government, but with no rails connecting to the fertile Salinas, Monterey would stay the crumbling and dilapidated Spanish capital she was now, instead of a thriving seaport town.

There was hard going after the narrow-gauge railroad was built. First a dry year, then 1877, when wheat, standing level with fence tops and in full milk, was pelted by an untimely rain so that thousands of acres went down in rust and did not yield a single sack of grain.

Carlisle Abbott mortgaged his San Lorenzo Rancho to keep the railroad going, and Jacks borrowed on more of his land. The narrow-gauge was bound to succeed, for it reduced the freight for rancheros, and money saved was money that talked loudest.

Passengers going to and from the county seat on business helped some and the Pacific Grove Methodist Retreat brought money in until too many of David Jacks's religious friends demanded passes and the company had to refuse free rides to all who were not officers or employees of the railroad. After this rule on the Monterey and Salinas Valley Railroad was enforced, a hard day came upon Carlisle Abbott, for the Reverend Mr. McGowan, an Episcopal clergyman, made a strong appeal for a pass and Abbott as well as Jacks wanted to advance religious affairs in the district. Mr. McGowan liked to travel often to Pacific Grove Retreat and he had so little money. Surely the "cloth" deserved something from business?

"No one but employees and officers of the railroad on passes." Mr. Abbott himself had put through the resolution.

Then God himself must have led the Canadian in good works. McGowan, if he was an employee, could ride free. That was easy. What the pitiful little railroad needed most was a chaplain! Abbott entered in his books the employment of the Reverend Mr. McGowan as chaplain of the Monterey and Salinas Valley Railroad Company and then handed the gentleman of the cloth his pass.

But not even a chaplain, praying twenty-four hours a day, could save the road from passing into the hands of receivers when the Southern Pacific saw too much freight going by narrow-gauge to Monterey to be shipped by boat to San Francisco. They reduced their freight rates below anything that would keep even a narrow-gauge in operation. This time money saved talked loudest for the opposition, and rancheros went Southern Pacific!

David Jacks dropped thousands of dollars when the Southern Pacific bought out the Monterey and Salinas at bankruptcy proceedings, and Carlisle Abbott lost his beautiful San Lorenzo Rancho as well as the land he had bought from Don David Spence. The Canadian left the Salinas Valley for Arizona, but the Scotchman stayed and took over more land from Mexicans and Californians on mortgages. He would soon make up his losses.

That other Scotchman David Spence had joined his ancestors, and his wife Adelaida Estrada followed him only a month later, which left the long-guarded Estrada-Spence holdings along the Salinas in the hands of their grandchildren, for their son's wife, Refugio Malarin, had already married again. But the old trader's dream, expressed in 1828, lived after him, a reality. He had said in those first days after he arrived in this golden land: "Any man can be a don in California, if he has land enough." Now, as mute evidence of his prophecy, there was chiseled in granite over his head in the cemeterio at Monterey the following words:

Don David Spence, born Huntley, Scotland, Oct. 1798, died, Monterey, California, 1875.

Idle ramblers in the cemeterio generations later would read the one-word success story of a poor Scotch salter and trader, who had prospered in California and turned don.

5

"Now Is Coming Trescony's Sheeps"

ALBERTO TRESCONY, the tinsmith at San Lucas Rancho, learned something in the dry year that ruined the Monterey and Salinas Valley Railroad. He saw and talked to Basques who had driven sheep from the San Joaquin Valley into the Salinas in search of pasture. There had been fights, plenty of them over grazing that year, with rancheros who owned great bands of cattle. Salinas vaqueros hustled many a Basque herder and his sheep back over the mountain passes at the point of a rifle.

These Basque herders were good people, gentle spoken, and they knew how to handle sheep. Trescony was having trouble with vaqueros and herders. The Chinese agitation, started in San Francisco sand lots, was causing reverberations in the Salinas. Already Trescony had been threatened by those who resented the Celestials. A committee waited upon him and told him that unless Chinks left his dairy ranch at Tularcitos the place would be burned to the ground and the Chinks roasted whole like the pigs they themselves ate on Chink New Year.

Sadhearted, Trescony let the faithful, hard-working Chinese go, to wander helpless in a hostile country and eventually to form tongs, or societies, for mutual protection, while they huddled together in squalor. Trescony rented out his Tularcitos.

But these Basques were men to know more about. The tinsmith talked long one day on a hillside with Echeverria, a Basque herder, while sheep nibbled at the dwindling pasture and heat waved across the dry valley. Echeverria had come from a place in the Basque country near the Spanish border. Many of his friends also had come to America, the big country where there was wide land and fewer people to live off pasture; America, where even a poor herder had a chance one day of owning land for himself.

Then the Basque explained to Trescony how he and his family and friends had come to California so far away from Europe. Rancheros in the San Joaquin had sent the passage money to be worked out in herding after their arrival. These rancheros had made great things possible for people of the Basque country.

The old tinsmith living alone on the rancho didn't ponder this opportunity long. Were there more Basques who would like to come to California? He could use some. There was land to be taken up from the government in the Salinas. Land the government *gave* to people, and he, Trescony, could use herders who were so good with sheep. It would not be hard, for he could speak Spanish and would treat them well.

And so it was that Alberto Trescony, the orphaned Italian tinsmith, started a stream of Basques toward the Salinas via boat to New Orleans, then to San Luis Obispo on the train, and finally over the grade by stage and into the land of promise. Pascale Balad, José Orradre from Navarre, and his brothers Miguel and Marsello, and Juan Gordo (fat John) Aniotzbehere and his brother Juan Flaco (lean John), good people all, who were to work hard and prosper and take up squatter's claims and government land, where their children and their children's children could be respected landholders and know happiness and freedom. Some of these faithful Basques worked for twenty to fifty years for the same "patron," even when they owned land of their own.

Trescony's children were now grown. The little motherless Julius was a young man, eighteen, in school at a place called St. Mary's College built on the sand dunes of San Francisco. This boy was on his own, with money enough to

ALBERTO TRESCONY'S TIN HOUSE TODAY

take care of his needs. Money from the fertile Salinas was giving the son of Alberto the education his father had never known. Young Julius would never have to carry everything in his head because he could not read or write!

And Rosa his daughter, too, had her share of happiness from sheep in the Salinas. She was married to Dr. Critsal and he, Alberto, had built them a fine house with thirteen rooms, in Santa Cruz across the bay from Monterey. This house had a bathroom with hot and cold water and an inside toilet that flushed! Rosa had two children now, an orchard and fine gardens. Yes, the Salinas had been good to Rosa, and to her sister too. All was going well with a tinsmith and his children.

Soon young Julius would be back from college, then perhaps he would marry and there would be little children to play once more in the beautiful adobe where Indians had marked crosses each day in the bricks.

Trescony treated the Basques well. No herder on Rancho San Lucas would know the old days of hardship the patron knew: days of lambing in the rain with only a brush shelter, and then the long ride home wet and tired and hungry. Alberto Trescony would see to that. With the aid of his trusty soldering iron and a trade learned long ago in Paris, he fashioned a fine movable sheep camp from discarded tins that had held sheep dip. It was a comfortable weatherproof tin home on wheels, with a chimney, that could be moved wherever the sheep might be grazing. The sheepherders of the San Lucas knew real luxury when winter winds howled through the Salinas and rain clattered against the tin.

Basques up and down the valley envied friends or relatives lucky enough to work at Trescony's, and when the camp was on the move, a cry went out at the sight of a tin house on wheels: "Now is coming Trescony's sheeps!"

Before long a sort of employment agency for Basque herders was established by old Alberto in San Francisco, where California rancheros in need of help were sure to find quiet gentle men from the Pyrenees. There was a Basque hotel in the center of town, where homesick ones who missed the colorful costumes and fiestas and the red and white houses of their homeland could talk and hear news from the timid newly-arrived who had been herded steerage into a boat and then shunted for days by train across the vast dry desert to California. For all Pyreneos there was comfort and good Basque food. The place was run by the Aguirres who had come from the Basque country by the way of Monte-video.

Here in the warm steaminess with the good smell of cooking, young Julius Trescony, sent by his father to procure a herder, met and loved on sight the sweet-voiced beautiful young Kate Aguirre who was eventually to fill the San Lucas adobe with the grandchildren old Alberto had dreamed about!

The tiny Kate was dainty as a doll and sang like a bird, but her father would not allow her to become a professional. Always there were bids for her songs. But old Aguirre would only let his Kate sing at the Spanish church for charity. San Francisco critics in papers hailed Kate Aguirre as another Adelina Patti, but her songs were ever to be lullabies sung to her babies in the adobe at Rancho San Lucas.

Old Alberto soon left management of the rancho with twenty thousand acres and twenty-five thousand sheep in the hands of young Julius, and went to live in Salinas at the Abbott House, the inn he had once bought with all its land for eight hundred dollars from Deacon Howe, son of the sewing machine man, and sold to Abbott who had lost it.

RANCHO SAN LUCAS CATTLE BRANDS

Alberto Trescony · *Julius Trescony* · *Rafael Estrada*

6

"Off with the Squatters!"   1878
The Great "Destierro"

WHILE Julius Trescony and his beautiful Kate
Aguirre lived their story of young love and contentment at
San Lucas Rancho, greed, heartaches, and poverty were im-
pressing themselves forever in the minds of one hundred and
ninety-three people at Jolon.

A few miles northwest of San Antonio Mission, where
once Ygnacio Pastor the Indian had peacefully tilled his Milpitas on land given him by padres, a frightful thing was
happening. Ygnacio's land had been sold to Faxon Atherton,
the father-in-law of young Gertrude Atherton, the novelist,
and now since the elder Atherton was dead, Gertrude and
her husband George had come down to manage this part of
the old man's estate.

Ygnacio Pastor had one league of land, the paper granting it said so, but somewhere along the line when the land
changed hands someone had calmly added another one to
Ygnacio's one league, creating an eleven-league rancho, forty-
two thousand instead of forty-two hundred acres! This was
simple, since there was no record of San Antonio Mission
lands being sold, and United States titles on land were hazy
to say the least. There was plenty of vacant land.

And now in 1878 George Atherton with his wife and

213

young baby had arrived at Jolon with two sheriffs and helpers to turn off those who lived on the land.

Fifty-three families consisting of one hundred and ninety-three souls were about to be dispossessed. Indians, Mexicans and Spaniards with small bits and ownership dating from Mexican occupation, and hard-working American citizens who had taken up little 160-acre pieces of "government" land in an effort to make a living in the wide fertile valley where Padre Junípero Serra had first raised the cross and cried out so joyously to men throughout the world.

The Athertons took rooms at the little stagecoach hotel in Jolon bordering on Milpitas Rancho, until some unfortunate family could be turned out of what they knew as home, and the place be cleaned up. Since the little inn was stuffy and the Athertons must leave the door open for air, a sheriff was posted outside to guard those who had come to bring sorrow and poverty into the San Antonio Valley!

The business of evicting began the next morning, and Gertrude Atherton stood in the doorway of the inn to watch the officers and men start out armed to the teeth.

At the first place (according to Mrs. Atherton) the evictors were met by six desperate farmers with rifles on their shoulders, but the officers and George Atherton swept aside those who struggled to protect all they possessed, marched into the house and flung the few sticks of furniture out of windows and doors, then set the shack ablaze!

No shots were fired. Perhaps this was because the recent owners were too numb at seeing all their worldly goods hurled so rapidly through the air. Sheriffs collected the defenders' guns before they recovered from their surprise.

Word traveled fast along the San Antonio, so that at several other farms there was no show of resistance. What was the use? These Athertons had money, lots of it. They lived on a fine estate not far from San Francisco, and they had brought sheriffs and guns. A poor man with a few acres could not stand up for his rights against this combination of power. Dispossessed men cursed but submitted, as ever the weak must give away to the powerful.

On went the plunderers, herding the half-naked men, women, and children before them, and burning shacks against the return.

As ever it had been in the Salinas region since the days of De Anza and his colonists, there was a Castro on hand! This Castro had the best house, and the Athertons took that over to live in. Castro was poor and helpless as the others, but he did not go down to defeat as easily as most. He made life miserable for George Atherton, who had taken his land and his home, by constantly dogging the conqueror, walking around him in circles gritting teeth and muttering threats until George was afraid to be alone lest Castro kill him.

Several days later, according to Gertrude Atherton's own well-told account, she drove over to the Mission San Antonio now in the middle of Atherton's rancho.

At San Antonio, according to Mrs. Atherton, "the squatters" had herded their families and livestock while they went off to seek hospitality elsewhere:

"It was a strange sight. The church and yard were crowded with women and children, sheep and goats. Winter was approaching, and it was very cold, but some immensely fat Mexican women wore but a single calico garment. The brown children, playing with goats, were stark naked. It was no warmer in the tottering church, and the first rain would add to their miseries.

"Mrs. Atherton, my mother-in-law, was a generous woman, but she knew as much about poverty as an infant in arms. I doubt if she had ever seen anyone poorer than a well-paid servant. For that matter there was no poverty in San Francisco at that time nor for many years later. But she felt that something should be done by the victor for the vanquished, and had given me a bolt of calico and two red flannel petticoats to give the dispossessed.

"This was the first time I had faced poverty and I was horrified. I could not see myself in role of 'Lady of the Manor' presenting something like fifty half-naked women and wholly naked children with a bolt of calico and two red petticoats as protection against bitter weather and compensation for all they had lost. I carried them back and the woman who kept the hotel made the presentation later."

The Athertons cleaned up Castro's house and sent for furniture, and George began to spend his time gambling at the inn at Jolon with a six-shooter on the table, while Gertrude stayed alone with her child and a Chinese cook, and listened to rain and the roar of the San Antonio River.

Castro came often to frighten her while George and the hired man were enjoying themselves at Jolon, and her nerves grew jumpy.

"One day, being frightened, I went to the kitchen where the Chinaman sat near the stove writing a novel.

" 'Fong,' I said, 'there are men on this ranch, bad ones as you know. They hate Mr. Atherton and might try to kill me. If I were in danger would you protect me?'

"His intelligent eyes suddenly went blank. 'No,' he said coldly. 'I do not fear death, why should you?' He shrugged his shoulders and waited politely until I left, before returning to what certainly looked like a work of art. Doubtless those long strips of flimsy yellow paper with their graceful hieroglyphics written for the most part in a lean-to with icy wind blowing through the cracks made him a famous author in China. Who can tell?" [1]

Not long after, Gertrude woke up one night. The river was only grumbling now and the wind had died down. She heard prowling footsteps and aroused George, who was cross

[1] From *Adventures of a Novelist* by Gertrude Atherton, published by *Liveright Publishing Corporation.*

at being awakened and claimed it was only coyotes. Then suddenly there was a terrific crash in the living room!

Fong, the Chinaman, sprang from his bed. One of the roof tiles lay on the hearth. It had certainly been flung down the chimney.

Gertrude threatened to leave, and George agreed! The Athertons, having possessed the disputed land, hired a manager for the ranch and moved out of the San Antonio away from the havoc they had wrought. But the memory of that great "Destierro" was to remain forever in memories of men and their children and their children's children in the Salinas. Not even the confirmation of title by the Supreme Court after twenty years of struggle could blot away hatred and resentment against the Athertons.

Not long after this terrible affair, a sad-faced nearly naked Indian rode into the plaza of San Lucas Rancho, left his horse by the barn and went in search of Don Julius Trescony.

Padre Doroteo Ambris, the faithful Indian priest, lay dead at San Antonio. Indians had no wood for a coffin for the priest they loved. Would Don Julius come and bring wood to make a coffin and maybe some black cloth to cover it? And would he, who understood about these things, tell the priest to come and pray for the peaceful rest of Padre Ambris, who wanted to be buried at the mission where he had worked for thirty years off and on?

Julius Trescony sent a vaquero up the Salinas to Mission San Miguel for the newly arrived parish priest whom the bishop had sent to raise money in an effort to save San Miguel from ruin; then, because he knew the small stature of old Doroteo Ambris, he had men on the rancho make a coffin. All helped to cover it with black. The young don started off over the wild hills to San Antonio with the coffin in a spring wagon and the priest beside him.

Cold February winds were biting, and rain lashed against their faces. Startled deer ran before them to disappear in the brush, rabbits popped out of sight and quail fluttered away, as if these wild things would not look upon the coffin of Ambris.

At the crumbling San Antonio they found the lifeless body of the last misionary priest, surrounded by a huddled little knot of sorrowing Indians.

But they could not bury Padre Ambris. He was not even decently covered, so tattered were his clothes! Once more young Julius set out over the hills; this time on horseback to town, where he bought blue jeans for a priest's burial and heard that the bishop from up north had learned about Padre Ambris's illness and was on his way to San Antonio.

And so it was that in new blue jeans the last Franciscan missionary, the Indian priest ordained at Santa Barbara, was buried with full honors by the bishop in the ruined Mission of San Antonio where he had labored so long and faithfully.

Cattle belonging to the Athertons wandered by and stopped. Soft brown eyes of the curious, lowing kine watched the proceedings a minute before they went on to nibble weeds around the ruined dooryard.

7

King's!

THERE WAS great excitement along the valley among "old ones" in the early eighties. A Frenchman had come, a poco loco Frenchman, a millionaire! He had purchased thirteen thousand acres of San Lorenzo grant which Abbott the Canadian had lost because the narrow-gauge railroad had failed. This new owner of San Lorenzo, Le Roi, whose father had translated the name to King instead of anglicizing it, had paid $105,000 for the land, with money he made by a monopoly of thousands of acres of redwood forests north of San Francisco.

Rancheros who ran cattle along the valley were laughing up their sleeves at this poco loco Frenchman, and they wished old Feliciano Soberanes who had once owned San Lorenzo Rancho was alive to laugh with them.

He was plowing up six thousand acres of land for dry-farming wheat, and using as many as one hundred and fifty horses at a time in eight-horse gangs of plows, seeders, and harrows.

This King the capitalist, so well-educated, who had traveled all over Europe and knew about horse racing, didn't know that it was far too dry at San Lorenzo for such farming. San Lorenzo was cattle land; it had always been cattle land since the days of the padres, and surely padres were wise men! This poco loco one was dizzy with land. He would walk out of the valley one day, as many others before him had done, leaving the land and plows for another.

Even if the wheat crop should grow and bear, how could so much grain be hauled miles and miles to Soledad on the San Vicente Rancho, where the railroad ended? It took ten mules to pull a load of wheat.

Poco loco was this King the dreamer. He had even brought from Germany a fool called Winterhalter, so-called expert who claimed sugar beets could be grown on King's land of Rancho San Lorenzo!

But the Salinas smiled on this new King, as ever fortune smiles on those who have riches and frowns on the poor. The wheat crop was tremendous and was hauled by team to Monterey where it was shipped by schooners. King the dreamer grew the richer for taking a chance.

Then Collis P. Huntington saw freight for his Southern Pacific Railroad in this vast business on King's rancho. The bright steel rails crept still farther up the valley through mustard and grain fields to "King's," where a little station was built on the rancho.

And with the railroad in, King soon shipped fine race horses down from his home rancho in the north. Three stallions came, which he had imported at three thousand dollars each. King built a schoolhouse and rented out wheat land to other farmers.

Two clever Americanos rented part of King's rancho that had brought eighty thousand bushels of wheat the year before and paid thirteen thousand dollars cash as rental. Then, without putting plow to furrow they took more than the rental off it in wild grain.

Old settlers along the Salinas went crazy with these big doings. A grain and milling warehouse was put up, and Ernest Steinbeck, father of young John who was one day to startle the world with his novels, was put in charge as mill man.

The grazing land Spaniards had granted to the long-dead Feliciano Soberanes was talking loud now with productivity.

King built a race track next, and his horses soon grew famous. Being French himself, he asked the French actress Sarah Bernhardt, now at the height of her career in Paris, to name his horses grown in the Valley of the Salinas, which she did in letters written by her own hand. But when he asked to have one called Sarah Bernhardt she refused flatly, saying that she'd die if she picked up a paper sometime and read in big headlines that "Sarah Bernhardt lost by a nose."

But there was disappointment too at King's. Winterhalter had failed in his experiments with sugar beets and, disgruntled, King told him he had better go back to Germany.

"Someday you will see," Winterhalter said in farewell, "someday this wide valley of the Salinas will have sugar beets growing and producing high sugar content. They *must* grow; they *will* grow, when some seed is found that will resist the terrible wind and tendency to rust." King only laughed, and the little German climbed into the smoky coal-burning train and returned heartbroken to Germany.

More farmers wanted land to plant in wheat, and then one day on a hill above his rancho King sat astride his horse and dreamed another dream. A town—King's City! Where now wind swept through the golden fields and great black crows cawed loudly even as they pilfered grain, there would one day be a city. He told his dream to young Birdie, daughter of his brother Lewis, who was beside him on her horse. She merely pulled her coat tighter in the wind and laughed.

Subdivision of the city came in 1887, and the townsite was laid out in the midst of a huge stubble field that had recently been burned over.

Charles King was not even discouraged by the lack of water. His new town waterworks was a well pumped in summertime by a windmill and in winter by a blindfolded mule who kept the tank filled. King City was a reality!

PART XI

A Teaspoonful of Brains Isn't Worth Much. 1889

Changes

OLD ALBERTO TRESCONY enjoyed living at Salinas City. There was so much doing now at the county seat, and with young Alberto and Julius and his family at San Lucas, the great rancho was in good hands. He had given land for right-of-way to the railroad that was being extended from King's City to San Lucas and already Julius was building the largest grain warehouse south of Salinas City. Lots in the newly surveyed San Lucas town were selling for $150 to $175 for 50 by 120 feet, and the church had bells blessed by the Jesuit priest of San Miguel. There was a store and a school for children of the sixteen tenant farmers who prospered on the land of an orphaned Italian tinsmith. His own grandchildren and their children's children would go to school in the town their own grandfather had founded near the three corners of his grants on the Salinas.

Civilization was marching fast up the valley now. Someday the railroad might even push on through the grazing land to Santa Margarita and maybe even over the great pass to San Luis Obispo and Santa Barbara. San Lucas town sixty miles south of Salinas City was bound to be a center.

To most of these new folks on the streets of Salinas City, the tall stoop-shouldered old man who lived at the Abbott House and played solitaire hour after hour in the bar, was an eccentric, a tipo! True, he did not eat eggs in winter when they were high, and several times, when he lost a day some-how in his calculations of the week and wore his best suit on Saturday instead of Sunday, he changed it quick lest it wear out. But then perhaps his mind had been thinking of the great changes in the valley during his twenty years.

From the mouth to the top, the wilderness of Salinas was different now. He could remember when Juan Bautista Castro had offered thirty-six thousand acres of his ranch for eighteen thousand dollars; only fifty cents an acre and not a taker. Now twenty-two hundred acres of that same land had recently sold for a hundred thousand dollars.

The Democrat Secessionist James Bardin, from Missis-sippi, had made good after the flood and paid squatters to take up more land for him at the river's mouth. He had brought in members of his family and staked them to land and a de la Vierra girl had married James Bardin's nephew. Old James had chuckled to Trescony only the other day because he had sold a piece of land and thrown in thirty extra acres of no-good bottoms for the buyer to pay taxes on!

Hartnell's widow, the little Teresa, was a clever one. She had somehow managed to get Hartnell's part of the Alisal back from David Jacks the moneylender, old adobe college and all. There was a mortgage on the Alisal, but Teresa had grown sons. Frisky colts they were and wild too, sowing oats from top to bottom of the valley, but they would help their mother.

Teresa's son Ulderico Hartnell had become county treas-urer after that other one, William Rumsey, was charged with taking thirty thousand dollars county money and even ac-cused of setting fire to the courthouse to cover his crime. But there were folks in Salinas who knew Rumsey was innocent. They knew also that county officials in need often tapped the county treasury to feed their families and that these same officials managed to be over in Monterey at a ball on the night the courthouse burned. William Rumsey didn't molder long in jail. He hired a good gringo lawyer and sent word to the proper people that if he was not released he would tell what he knew. In no time Rumsey was out and away from the region and nothing more was said about the courthouse fire.

Rafael Estrada who had charmed Cristina Delgado into giving him her land after he had lost his own, had walked off the last of Delgado land at the river's mouth with his wife Isabel Malarin, the remainder of their children, and six hundred dollars. He had bought back a 150-acre piece of Guadalupe Rancho that they had lost long ago.

Ignacio's giddy-headed actress wife was now only a hectic memory. Through the careful management of his nephew Ramón Somavia, Ignacio Malarin had managed to retrieve his interest in Guadalupe, and he was living contentedly with his second wife, the beautiful Anita Vanderhurst.

Farther up, where the Malarins had owned so much land, there were changes with this great flow of civilization. *Many* farmers were packed into land where once Estrada and Malarin cattle had roamed. Swiss farmers had poured into the valley penniless, to work as hired hands, and they stayed on to buy or rent land of their own for dairy farms.

On Urbano's share of Buena Vista Rancho, lost because of gambling with the Frenchman, a German emigrant from Hanover, Claus Spreckels, was trying out sugar beets, and talked of great crops and a sugar refinery in the Salinas. This Claus Spreckels was rich now, with many refineries which had stemmed from his experimental place up near San Francisco. But old Alberto Trescony thought of that other German, Winterhalter, at King's place who had tried sugar beets in the Salinas and failed because of curly top, a beet blight, and how he had left the valley broken hearted. Alberto only went on in silence playing solitaire and wondering what toys to take for Julius's children when they talked big about sugar beets in the Salinas.

Malarins didn't live on the land. They had only Guadalupe left now. Mariano with his rich wife Lola Pacheco stayed in Monterey except for summers, and just recently a "catch colt" of Francisco Pacheco's had led them to thirty thousand dollars that the old man had hidden behind adobe bricks in the wall. Salinas Valley crops were keeping Mariano's daughters, and the husbands they had met in Spain, in luxury in San Francisco.

Swiss farmers and Danes were now on Jacks land that Mariano had lost and that the old Peruvian trader Juan Malarin had loved. The Swiss farmers made a good living and had money in the bank from just farming on shares. There was a record that year of two hundred bushels of wheat to the acre. Madre de Dios, how the old Peruvian trader would turn over in his grave if he knew about that, and all this money out of his family.

Young David Spence had only a summer place on the land his grandfather, the Scotch salter turned don, had cherished. Young David was a fine fellow living in San Francisco while Swiss farmers and Danes tilled his land and filled the warehouses with grain at Spence's Switch.

Soledad town flourished on Esteban Munras's rancho San Vicente, not by the labor of Don Esteban's children, but by Danes and Swiss who tilled the land, bought in the stores, sent their children to the school, and attended the church.

The Bianchinis and Fransconis and Dedinis and Petersons and Iversons and Sorensens were good folk all, and hard workers on the land, and they had prospered in ten years along the Salinas.

The Swiss were good at love too. Clotilde Soberanes, daughter of Francisco and granddaughter of old Feliciano, had married a handsome Swiss farmer, Bianchi. But there was trouble now among the Soberanes brothers, a fight over what land was left. Francisco was dead, and his widow, the gentle little Isabel Boronda, had given her share of land to her favorite unmarried son Abel. Another son, Benito, felt this was an injustice because his mother's share of land should not go to one child alone, but be divided among all Francisco's children. In the courts Benito declared the old lady incompetent.

All the town was talking about this lawsuit between brothers from the same mother. Some said Benito was right, and some said Benito was wrong. The papers were full of the affair. Old Trescony couldn't read papers so he went to the trial.

The Judge, Dorn, was a good man and just. This was not a matter for one man alone to decide. There would be a jury trial.

When the judge asked old Mrs. Soberanes to count on her fingers, her black eyes had snapped with anger. She told him she was no Indian. "If you want me to count, give me some *money* to count, dollars and quarters and such, and I'll soon show you!"

Then the attorneys for the brothers who were fighting her asked: "Mrs. Soberanes, if you were given three dozen eggs to take to the store for sale, and they were thirty-five cents a dozen, how much would you get for them?"

The white-haired old lady smiled, and her black widow's bonnet tipped up proudly. "My husband never had *me* peddling eggs."

When all had testified, the jury went out. Each side rested confidently in the knowledge that justice would come back sure and strong in the decision of those twelve men good and true.

The verdict was given. The jury shook hands with the valiant old lady and went home. Benito had lost the case.

If that could have been the end to trouble, if it only could! But lawyers as usual got the lion's share, and Benito had to mortgage land for the money to fight. Then one morning Abel had gone out to shoot rabbits and did not return. The woman who kept his house was worried. They found Abel dead, with a bullet in his brain and the gun against his head.

The coroner called Abel's death suicide, but the coroner had given notes for money he had borrowed from Abel and the notes were never found. Even Indians in the valley knew that a gun kicks back and would not be against the head if it had been fired by the dead person!

"Uncle Abel" was missed, for he always had a kind word and pressed fifty-cent pieces into the grubby hands of little children.

As he put a red ten on a black jack, old Alberto Trescony smiled with satisfaction. There would be no fight over his property after he was gone. He, a man of little learning, had spent long hours to figure out a will that would hold; a lawyerproof will, to protect his children and their children. There was sadness when he thought of the little children Rose Cristal had left when she died only a bit ago, just a month after giving birth to her only boy Leo Cristal. Those children of Rose Trescony and all the rest would be looked after well when Alberto's bones moldered in a cemetery and his land was divided.

Prosperity was moving fast along the Valley of the Salinas now that the railroad had opened things up.

King's City was growing, and through King's efforts the county had voted a bond issue to bridge the Salinas; a hundred and fifty thousand dollars for four bridges. One bridge would be not far from Salinas City on the road to Monterey on Buena Vista Rancho, one at Soledad on San Vicente, and a great long one at King's City; the last, to the south of his own San Lucas.

Old Trescony, sitting in the warmth of the Abbott House, thought about this great improvement. He could remember the hazardous stage crossings when quicksand changed in the river bed within a few hours; of the Indian vaquero drunk on his way home, who missed the crossing and disappeared, horses, wagon and all!

To the south of San Lucas on the big San Bernardo once owned by Mariano Soberanes, brother to Feliciano, a rich Jew, Brandenstein, and his partner Gotchaux had three thousand cattle and a little settlement called San Ardo. He had been a crafty one, had the Jew. Besides selling high the right-of-way for the railroad, instead of giving it, he had made the company agree to stop all trains at his boxlike shelter in the wilds.

Brandenstein, the wholesale butcher from San Francisco, had fenced his San Bernardo with fifty miles of showy white pickets, and had formed the San Bernardo Canal and Irrigation Company and dug a great canal to carry three feet of water from the Salinas River to irrigate five or six thousand acres of his ranch. But it had cost him twenty thousand dollars! The old padres had been smarter than a Jew, with their Indian labor working on irrigation ditches.

Brandenstein planned soon to divide the place into small parcels for farmers.

And next to the Jew and not far from San Miguel, on land of San Bernardo that had been turned back to the government in the title shake-up, was Manuel Alessandro, the Portuguese whaler who had given up the hard life of the sea for an even harder life as a sheep and cattle man. Alessandro, the Portuguese, and his sheep had already won the first battle with his neighbor the Jew.

Brandenstein's foreman had refused to let the Portuguese drive his sheep through San Bernardo along the river bottom, to stubble fields he had rented beyond. But young Manuel had been to school; he knew where to go and what to do. He visited the land commissioner at Salinas City and found that, since there was no county road and the river bottom belonged to the government, it could be used legally by any citizen as a highway along which to drive sheep or cattle so long as the animals didn't go on the land. Never again would ranchers of the Salinas have to pay foremen for the privilege of driving animals through another's property.

The land was in many hands now; land that was a vast wilderness of mustard when Alberto Trescony arrived in the Salinas. People had come from all over the world, and each laborer who came brought hands to work and brain to think, and that helped all the rest of the folks in the wide Salinas. Many people and prosperity.

Irish Griffins, from Dublin, were prospering now in Priest Valley where Kit Carson and Joe Walker had seen Padre Ambris kneeling in prayer with his Indians. French people had settled with their families in a valley to the west that they had named Paris Valley.

There were Basques, the Aniotzbeheres to the south of Trescony's own place, who had taken up government land and were now well-to-do, and Basques even renting land of San Lucas and farming on shares.

An Irishman, Murphy, had Atascadero Rancho and Santa Margarita at the head of the valley that had once been the pride of the free-spending Estradas.

At San Miguel, where sandaled Franciscans in brown homemade robes once labored along with Indians, the All-Seeing Eye looked upon a Jesuit priest who lived in quarters where Reed had been murdered, and was raising money to repair the termite-infested beams, in an effort to save the old building.

There were few Indians left around Jolon, and Atherton's manager Roberto Diaz had taken statues and relics from the ruins of San Antonio to save them. Brown, a butcher of San Francisco, had the Milpitas Rancho, and the hooves of his hogs clacked over the unmarked graves of Padre Sarria and Padre Ambris inside the church.

Alberto was thankful that his son Julius was good to Indians, and had sent a carpenter and wood to put a roof over the San Miguel to save what was left. Indians knew they had friends among the Tresconys at Rancho San Lucas.

This kindness to Indians had recently made young Julius the butt of a joke that rang through the streets of Salinas City. "The patron," Don Julius, had come into court to help a frightened San Antonio Indian woman who worked on the ranch. When they put her on the witness stand and the judge asked her how many children she had, the Indian woman shouted the length of the courtroom, "How many children have we, Don Julius?" The boy would never live down that tale!

What would padres who had Christianized Indians and built missions think now of the valley wilderness they had first settled? Salinas City alone had several hundred people and even an "Eastern doctor" to take business away from old black-whiskered Spanish midwives.

This new doctor was a clever Americano. Only recently he had been called to the New Indria quicksilver mine where a shooting scrape had put a bullet into the head of old Antonio who was not too bright. The doctor boiled a teaspoon, scooped up the brains that had leaked out, cleaned up the wound, and old Tony was brighter now than he had ever been in all his life! With some folks a teaspoonful of brains was worth more out of their heads than in.

2

Old Man of the River Is Dead. 1890

"GABRIEL'S DEAD!" "Old Gabriel lived to be a hundred and fifty-one, but now he's dead!"

The news traveled fast. Gabriel of the seven wives; Gabriel the Indian who had helped to build Salinas missions that were now ruins was dead.

In stuffy little dressmaking parlors of Salinas City, "modistes" thought of the frail stooped old man with a cane who came to beg bright-colored scraps from them to sew on his many-colored coat; how he had tipped his "plug" hat so politely and tied the bits in his bandanna, happy as a child. The photographers, Frank Bacon and his brother, remembered well how frightened Old Gabriel was the first time they took his picture. He fought them, thinking he was to be shot! Then when he saw his own likeness on paper he was delighted. After that he climbed the stairs to their "studio" by himself to "pose" for them. Now, with Gabriel dead, they looked through their files in an effort to "cash in" on their pictures of Old Gabriel—the pictures that Father Sorrentine had sent to the Pope in Rome with affidavits.

Telegraph wires flashed! Newspaper people in San Francisco as well as Salinas looked in morgues for material about the oldest man on record.

For the San Francisco *Examiner* men, there was a big scoop. They had a story written only a year ago, when

OLD GABRIEL

Gabriel at one hundred and fifty years had gone on the warpath with a knife.

San Francisco Examiner April 21, 1889.
Older Than The Union
An Indian Who Has Lived a Century and a Half.
Baptized By Junipero

The Story of Old Gabriel, Who Had Grandchildren
Before the Revolution

"One day last week an old Indian applied for admission to the Monterey County Hospital. He was given a bath and a meal, and as nothing but the feebleness of years seemed to be the matter with him he was allowed to wander about the grounds. After passing from one place to another he stopped to peer through the windows of one of the rear buildings.

"On the cot next to the window Old Gabriel, whose marvelous age has made him famous, lay. He turned his rheumy eyes upward and saw the dark face peering in on him.

"Old Gabriel, with a wild yell, dropped the coat on which he was sewing bright-colored patches, grabbed the knife that he has carried ever since the old missionaries brought it to California, and sprang to his feet.

"The old Indian looking in at the window saw the threatening aspect of Gabriel and fled. Before Old Gabriel's tottering legs had brought him to the door the other Indian had disappeared. He was soon on the road to Salinas.

"Old Gabriel stood at his door muttering angrily. A turn of the road is in sight of the door, and when the newcomer reached this turn Old Gabriel saw him again. He repeated the ugly yell with which he had greeted the other's first appearance. Then he returned to his cot, gathered up the blankets, tied them with a stout cord to his shoulders, and with his knife in his hand stealthily left the hospital grounds and was soon on the road.

"Some of the other patients, however, saw him go, and told the steward, who went after to bring him back. Gabriel had not more than fifteen minutes' start, and yet the steward had gone nearly a mile before he caught up with him.

"The old man was getting over the ground in a swinging trot that hardly raised the dust. He still held his knife in his hand and his eyes were fastened on the figure of a man half a mile ahead.

"Old Gabriel never heeded his pursuer until the latter had overtaken him.

"Then he turned, and snarled angrily. When the steward placed himself in the road ahead of him and motioned him to return, he gave vent to some uncouth sounds, seemingly a protest in the Indian language against being compelled to return. When he finally saw that it was no use objecting, he turned and sullenly hobbled back to his cot.

"An attempt was made, but without success, to find the other old Indian, who looked as old as Gabriel, but, unlike him, could speak intelligently in Spanish.

"Gabriel was questioned as to the reason of his animosity, but, though he seemed to understand what was wanted, only grunted:

"'Um! um! no bueno. Muy malo, mal Indio.'

"Then he struck into his native tongue again and no one could understand what he said.

"How long ago did this quarrel begin? What started it? It is half a century ago since the tribes were scattered and it must have been before that.

"In 1769 the good Padre Junipero Serra landed at Monterey and old Gabriel, even then a grandfather, was the first to be baptized by the missionary.

"Whether this Indian stole Gabriel's first sweetheart, or

slew his brother, or robbed him of the carcass of a deer, the injury has rankled more than a century.

"How old is Gabriel? He cannot tell; but by the events he describes and the recollections of people long since dead he must be at least 150 years old. He may be much older.

"This seems impossible, but no one in that part of the country conversant with the facts doubts it.

"Father Sorrentine, the parish priest of Salinas, has ever since his arrival in Monterey county, nearly forty years ago, taken a great interest in the old Indian. He says that there can be no doubt that Gabriel has turned his third half century.

'In 1854,' said Father Sorrentine, 'when I arrived at Monterey with Bishop Amat, we were met and welcomed by a number of Indians. They were captained by old Gabriel, who was even then the oldest among them. They gave his age as 110 years.

'I soon got to know Gabriel very well. He was then living with his sixth wife, and had children by her.

'The statements of his people in regard to his great age attracted my attention to him and I began to question him about events that occurred in the last century.

'The landing of Father Junipero Serro he remembered perfectly. I merely mentioned the name "Junipero", when his face lighted up and he gave me a full account of the event—how the priest landed and performed his first mass under a tree, and how he baptized this man first, giving him the name of Gabriel, and then the others of his tribe. He pointed out the spot where Father Junipero landed at Monterey, and mentioned other incidents which I have since forgotten.

'Now, if he was not there, how came this old ignorant Indian to know of historical events of which even educated white people, unless they have made the subject a special study, know nothing?

'When the missionary landed, Gabriel had buried his first wife and taken a second, and his children's children were living near him.

'Only a few years ago I spoke to Gabriel about these early events. Though he speaks no English and but little Spanish, he indicated his recollection of all of them.

'I think there is no doubt that the story of his baptism is correct.

'The Carmelo mission was established in 1770 or 1771, and Gabriel made adobes for the erection of the chapel. He did the same sort of work on the mission buildings at Soledad and San Antonio, which were erected under the direction of Father Junipero.

'All of these adobe chapels have been obliterated but the adobe maker still lives.

'Gabriel was taught to cut stones, and so was one of the principal workmen when the new Carmelo mission was erected about 1791.

'I have reason to believe the truth of all this. I once gathered all the evidence I could find on the subject of this man's age, and forwarded the affidavits to Rome.

'The mother of Manuel Castro, ex-Tax Collector of Salinas, who died a few years ago, aged ninety-five years, told me that when she was a child five or six years old at Monterey she knew this Indian, and that even then he was gray and wrinkled and was known, as now, by the name Old Gabriel.

'Dona Catarina Moras, when she was within a year or two of 100, told me the same thing.

'While Gabriel was in the Sotaville Hospital he had for a roommate another old Indian, who had known him all his life and who subsequently died at the age of 115. Some time before his death I asked him old old Gabriel was.

'He answered, with a grimace:

' "*Gabriel era viejo quando yo estaba muchacho*" (Gabriel was an old man when I was a boy).

'Few men have led as virtuous a life as this old Indian. To each wife he was married with all formality and he lived faithful to each one of the seven until she died.

'He has never indulged in any sort of excess. As for tobacco and liquor, he has never touched either.

'He is a good Catholic and until a year or so ago attended church regularly. He used to come into the church and shout to me from the door that he wanted a place, and I would always find a chair for him in front.

'He is said to have had children by every one of his wives, but they have all disappeared. An Indian known as Zacharias, who was probably one hundred years old, was said to be his son. I once asked Zacharias if this were true, but he answered:

"*Yo no se quien es me padre*" (I don't know who is my father).

'They say old Gabriel is losing his mind and his memory, but I think that he is only a little sullen, as he does not like his present surroundings. When he was at the Sotaville Hospital he was happy, bright and talkative. He and his old roommate chatted and sewed from morning until night, but now that there is no one around whom he knows or can talk to, he is dissatisfied and silent.'

"Old Gabriel was visited at the hospital. He was found in bed with his clothes on. He paid no attention when his name was called, but on being touched the blankets came down and revealed a face black as a negro's and seamed and furrowed in every direction with a thousand little wrinkles. His small eyes and abnormally thick under lip, and the aimless manner in which he rubbed the back of his wrists across his face suggested something of a large ape. The continual movements of the heavy black under lip made this resemblance more striking. The lip drooped and showed half a dozen fairly sound teeth.

"His short hair was gray, not white, and as thick as that

of a boy. He sat up watching his visitors suspiciously. Years ago Gabriel is said to have been six feet high. Now he is hardly five feet four, though his shoulders are not bent and he carries his head erect. His hands probably indicate more than any of his features his great age. They are black, bony and wrinkled; the flesh has shrunk away from his finger-nails and the ends of his thumb and forefinger, between which he holds his needle when he sews, are calloused cavities.

"When a camera was placed before him he grew very uneasy and seemed afraid. Suddenly he seemed to remember and to comprehend what was wanted, for he made an effort to straighten his clothes and to pose. When he was taken out to be photographed two years ago he concluded that he was to be shot, as he was so old, and fought strenuously. After it was over and he was shown the picture, he understood and chuckled over his fright.

"While the hospital attendants were present he would not even look up when spoken to. He preserved this manner for a time when the EXAMINER man was alone with him. After trying by various means to rouse him the visitor took something from his pocket.

" 'Dulces,' he called into the old man's ear.

"Gabriel turned sharply and grabbed the pieces of candy. He fairly shouted with joy and he pushed them into his mouth.

"This broke the spell. He put on an old stovepipe hat and insisted on shaking hands over and over again.

" 'Me Gabriel,' he exclaimed proudly, 'Gabriel, Capi-tán.'

"He is said to have been chief of a tribe of Tulare Indians when the missionaries came to this Coast.

"Then he began to mumble unintelligibly.

" 'Padre Junipero,' said the visitor, taking a hint from Father Sorrentine's story.

"The old man's little eyes lighted up again.

" 'Junipero,' he repeated excitedly, throwing his arms around his head, 'Junipero me, me!—babtisa me.'

"He indicated with his hands the ceremony of baptism and then crossed himself and fell to muttering prayer.

"The mention of Carmelo brought him again out of his lethargy.

"He repeated the name of the Mission and then stooped, and with his hands imitated the motions of one making *adobes,* speaking all the time rapidly in his Indian tongue, with an occasional Spanish word, from which his meaning could be gathered.

"His tongue once loosed he went on at a rapid rate.

"He seemed to be inveighing against the people of the various towns of the section. What could be understood of his mutterings translated into English ran something like this:

" 'Salinas, Soledad, Carmelo, Monterey. Many people there now. They are nothing! I! I am the man! I am a captain —chief. I was here before they were born. I am the oldest.'

"Then he fell to muttering again: *'Viejo, viejo, viejo.'*

"The old man's dinner was brought to him and he immediately forgot his visitor and began to eat. He buttered his bread and dipped it into his soup. He soon discarded his spoon and knife and fork and drank the soup from his bowl. A mutton chop and a potato he ate with apparent relish.

"All this time he seemed oblivious of any one's presence, but when the visitor started to leave he turned suddenly and extended his withered hand.

" 'Adios,' he said.

"Old Gabriel weighs 121 pounds, and his limbs are full and strong.

"He has always been very particular about bathing, and when he was active had a sweatbox on the banks of the stream near which he lived. Now that he is unable to bathe as often as he would like, he strips himself every day or two and with his old knife scrapes his skin from head to foot, thus keeping the pores open and his skin healthy.

"He will take no medicine whatever, but whenever he is at all ill he scrapes harder than usual, and makes the blood run. This seems to relieve him.

"Once Dr. Archer, the County Physician, tried to get him to drink a glass of brandy, but the old Indian snarled at him and pushed the liquor away with such vigor that it was thrown to the floor.

"The old man walks feebly, but without other assistance than a stick. His eyes are good, and he eats three meals a day.

"For years his sole employment has been sewing. He sews one patch after another of bright-colored cloth onto his coat and trousers, until they look as if they were pieces of a crazy quilt.

"The Indians all attribute Gabriel's longevity to his having been the first to submit to the priest's baptism.

"Mrs. W. J. Johnson, wife of the Salinas banker, for whose family old Gabriel worked many years, was asked what she knew of the old man.

"He was, she said, as honest as the day, and as faithful as a watchdog. When he got too old to work she cared for him, and so probably became better acquainted with him than any one living. But even she cannot converse with the old man freely, as he has forgotten nearly all the Spanish he learned in his prime, and only his mother language is left him. The habits and associations of his early savage life survive all he learned. He discarded his clothes and stalked around naked as when he was a young brave. So she could keep him no longer. At the hospital, however, she frequently visits him. Mrs. Johnson and the good parish priest are the only friends the old man has left. Poor old Gabriel! Had George Washington lived until this day he would hardly have been older.

"He has outlived his people and their time. He has outlived even his language."

The San Francisco *Chronicle* had a two-column story of an interview with the old man, given eight months after the *Examiner* article.

The Sacramento *Bee* printed the county aid claim from the state controller's office for $544.37, for a man who dated from George Washington's time!

Dr. Archer, the health officer of Salinas City, was anxious too. He wanted to perform an autopsy on this man with three half centuries to his credit! What made Old Gabriel's works tick longer than those of any other man on record? Archer was convinced after considerable study that Gabriel was a San Antonio Indian, and not a Tulare Indian as reporters claimed.

The doctor had his wish. He was privileged to see inside Old Gabriel, now that the "works" had stopped forever. The report of his autopsy is as follows:

"Lungs less than normal. All other organs atrophied— particularly the liver. The weight of that was 24 ounces, when it should have been 50 to 60. Had only one tooth. Heart irrespective of the condition of the aorta was normal except for a little fatty degeneration. Abdominal cavity atheromatous degeneration. Gall bladder distended and contained very little bile. Almost no blood in cadaver. Very little ossification of cartilage, such as a surgeon would find in a child."

Benito Soberanes, great-grandson of that first young soldier José Maria Soberanes, who had dreamed of land in the Salinas, was a pallbearer for Old Gabriel who had known the first Soberanes at Soledad when he worked on the mission.

3

Special to San Lucas

SLANTING rays of October sun warmed golden hills of the Salinas. At the county seat the black-draped engine of a "special" was headed south for San Lucas.

Alberto Trescony was dead! The orphaned Italian tinsmith who had once walked thousands of miles across Mexico to sell his sheep, now lay white and still, waiting to ride in state with a trainful of mourners behind him. There would be services at the little burying ground perched high above the river on a hill to the east, and looking over the valley at the three boundary corners of Trescony's own land. The cemetery the old man had laid out himself, with the steel rails of the railroad running just below. The whole of the Pleasant View Hotel was in readiness for the funeral party at San Lucas, and there would be food and drink for all. Old Alberto, the thrifty one who once hired an Indian to gather wool that sheep left on fences, had wanted it thus.

A motley crowd stood bareheaded in the wind to pay last respects to the tinsmith before yellow soil of his beloved valley covered him with a final blanket.

There were Indians in clean but faded blue jeans, who had left their work in the fields to bid their patron good-bye forever, and paisanos he had helped with good advice and an occasional bit of money; Spaniards and Mexican vaqueros complete with silver-trimmed jackets usually worn to fiestas, mingled with the fine folks from San Francisco and Monterey in their silks. Brunetti, the Italian whom Trescony had set up in a hotel of his own in King's City, was there; and Basque herders; Danes and Swiss he had befriended and who had affection for the queer soft-spoken old man. And there were grown folk who as children in Monterey had cherished tin cups he had made over his little fires in the street.

All these bowed their heads as the body was lowered so that old Trescony would ever look up the valley he had loved.

But scarce were the tinsmith's bones cold in their new bed before trouble brewed. Dr. Cristal, the widower, father to Rose Trescony's children, began court proceedings to con test Alberto's will on the grounds of undue pressure or influence, and even sanity, because he thought his children were not getting enough of their grandfather's money. Dr. Cristal accused young Julius and his sister Teresa Johnson, of these things; and because of dry years with loss of crops, young Julius had to put a mortgage on San Lucas to get ready cash for fighting the case. Once more there was a field day for lawyers over twenty thousand acres of land in the fertile Salinas.

The result of that trial: The will was sustained and the estate divided as the testator wished. All would go well now for the Tresconys, with old Alberto's lawyer-tight will standing as he had written it.

4

Culture and Courts Bloom in the Salinas

IN 1895 Deacon Howe, who had thirty-nine years before owned the tavern in the mustard, wrote back from Mill River, Massachusetts. He was sorry about the drought that had attacked the Salinas, and startled to hear of all the changes around his place at the crossroads, where now over two thousand people were living. He didn't like Massachusetts. After all, there was too *much* water at Mill River and not enough whisky, and the panic had hit hard among millworkers. He wished he had stayed under clear blue California skies where he could watch fields of wild flowers come into bloom even if there were no stages to race to his dooryard.

Flowers still bloomed in the Salinas Valley, but culture as well was bursting its buds to flower in Salinas City.

The Woman's Christian Temperance Union had started a place to rent books for fifty cents a month—a place called a public library where there was good clean reading. Something was doing now at least one night a week in the county seat.

Professor Bell had come to lecture on "Love, Courtship and Marriage" and also would give an evening on "Shame," but mostly women went to his lectures. It was suspected among husbands who gambled in the saloons while their wives "cultured" themselves that at least part of the audience went to see who else in town could be interested in such subjects.

Bill Nye Jr. was on the lecture platform, too, according to the bills put at doors and a notice in the paper: "He lectures on whatever he thinks about or what the occasion requires," which in Salinas was mostly making fun of Professor Bell's "Shame" and "Love and Marriage." The hall where Bill Nye spoke was always packed with men who wanted a good laugh, but who must return home to the sour visages of their wives who thought lectures were to *improve* the mind.

Then there was the young photographer Frank Bacon and his brother. Frank just couldn't keep his mind on the sitters and on adjusting the steel braces to their heads, for thinking about play acting. The little velvet-hung "studio" was always littered with papers that Frank said were the play he was writing.

Spanish Californians dressed in their best stiff silks and ready to be posed tapped their heads and shrugged their shoulders when he told them about the play. Frank Bacon was poco loco on the play-acting business. He had formed a dramatic society to play Nat Goodwin's *Turned Up,* and filled the hall. Now Frank was worse than ever. He had pulled a dark cloth over the camera and told his brother that it was "curtains" for photography. Then he went off to be an actor.

Poor Frank, he had been able to arrange a dress so well into folds to bring out the best in silk, for a picture, and children had smiled when he made faces, in spite of stiff starched panties pricking their bottoms and a steel brace holding their heads.

The days at the courthouse were even more thrilling

than the culture and shows of the night. From January to December it was a busy year for lawyers in Salinas City.

In January David Jacks and other great landowners started the ball rolling by appearing at the courthouse to plead with the Board of Equalization to reduce taxes on large landholdings, and the papers were full of resentment over their plea.

"Why should these land grabbers who obtained their holdings from Spaniards for a song have reduced taxes because they owned so much?" demanded the editor of the Salinas City *Owl*. "Their land was made valuable by poor men who improved small farms nearby and paid taxes for roads and such. Large owners should pay taxes at the same rate as if it were cut up into small farms. Unimproved land was no excuse. It only puts a premium on not doing anything with the land."

Small taxpayers were up in arms over this great injustice that the big owners proposed to put through. In Salinas City there was rabble-rousing among Spaniards and Mexicans who had lost their land through unfair practices. One Spaniard who had been turned off his land by Jacks and called a "squatter" took a shot at Jacks but missed, and he cooled his ardor in San Quentin—perhaps for life.

David Jacks kindly offered carriages for the Board of Equalization to ride and see his lands, which made the *Owl* editor do some sleuthing and give publicity to the doings of a moneylender.

"When David Jacks owned all of tracts Number Two of Monterey City lands, that section was permitted to remain unproductive. Some time ago Surveyor Garbor of Salinas, employed by the Government, discovered that Jacks had fenced 700 acres of Government land that did *not* belong to him; land which was open to settlement. Jacks then managed to place squatters on most of it, but others got in and settled portions of it. One has only to look at the contrast between Jacks and the settlers. It is apparent. Vineyards, beans, peaches. Does anyone need to prove that large land holders are a curse to the community?

"If Mr. Jacks or any other land-grabber does not care to pay just tax on the vast possessions which they are occupying to the exclusion of others, let them cut up and sell it at a reasonable figure and there will be plenty to buy them who will pay taxes without a kick."

David Jacks the canny Scotchman did not give up because of the free press and public opinion. He claimed to be "land poor" and asked that a special commission be appointed to investigate his lands. But many of the officials in the county seat were old-timers, who had suffered at the hands of the moneylender, and they knew well that he intended to use pressure, so they deemed a special committee unnecessary, because, "Any private citizen making a decision *against* Jacks would suffer—hence we see the reason for private citizens being asked to serve on this 'special' commission, when there is in existence a land commission Board of Equalization perfectly able to do the same work, but who *cannot* be influenced."

The sharp practices of David Jacks from Crieff had at last caught up with him. For the first time since his arrival defeat was his porridge to eat.

A little band of dispossessed Mexicans and Indians who huddled together in a tumbled-down adobe, smiled when they were told, for now Jacks had five children, and they had put a curse on him that never would his seed of greed spread to another generation. He would have no grandchildren. So far the curse was holding! Perhaps the Christian God was working as well as the pagan god in the case of this Jacks, who gave money for colleges and great lenses to see the stars—Jacks had been giving away money that he gained from land he had taken from Mexicans and Indians along the Salinas.

The next day in court, Atacio Campos, a bronze native son of the Salinas, was acquitted for stealing a cow, even though a piece of Campos's lasso stayed on the animal's neck when her owner found her! *Intent* of the crime had failed to be established. Yes, the court was a thrilling place in Salinas City that year.

Just before Thanksgiving, a great sensation struck. A big blond "city" lawyer came and took a seat at the hearing of the report from trustees of the estate of Alberto Trescony, in regard to the minor children of Dr. Cristal.

When the report ended, this large, blond Mr. Mitchell got to his feet. Instead of one-third of Alberto Trescony's estate, the Cristal children should get the whole of it!

The demand of this man shocked everybody in the courtroom to silence, and then Mr. Mitchell told all present that the *Supreme Court* of the United States had decided in the Wakerly case *against* perpetuities, and, as all bequests in the Trescony estate *were* perpetuities *except* those of the Cristal children, the children should inherit the whole of Alberto Trescony's twenty thousand acres of land. In the will he left Alexander Rainey, stepson, and wife one thousand acres for life, the absolute ownership to fall to their children. The remainder of the estate was divided into three parts: 1. Julius Trescony and wife for life and then to their children. 2. Teresa H. Johnson in like manner, and the residue to go *directly* to the children of Dr. Cristal. Hence it was plain to see that the Cristal children were the only direct inheritors!

Hard-working Julius was startled as if a thunderclap had struck. Was this man Cristal, who had gone away from Rose to Ireland for years and then returned when he was ready, and produced a third child, to get all the land because of this legal technicality? SUPREME COURT! Final court of the land!

Another mortgage went onto San Lucas Rancho, and

the long and costly lawsuit to protect Alberto's other children and grandchildren was started in the courthouse at Salinas City.

The old tinsmith's carefully worded lawyer-proof will was torn to pieces by greed, and his land mortgaged to pay for the tearing. This on top of the dry year of 1894!

Madre de Dios, but the court was a busy place! On December 15th a novel suit was filed by lawyers on behalf of a minister of the gospel against David Jacks the Scotchman, who, in one of his religious moods agreed with the people of Palo Alto in the Santa Clara Valley, to donate one thousand dollars for a Presbyterian church there. The people, believing in his honesty, went ahead and built, then Jacks gave only five hundred dollars and now the minister of the poor little church was bringing suit for the remainder of the money.

There was money trouble for Benito Soberanes. Lawyers' fees to fight his brother, Abel, and the dry year had put a great debt on Benito's rancho that he could not hope to pay, and the bank held the mortgage.

Benito was frantic. To think he must lose the land now when everything was set to make real money on the rancho. Claus Spreckels, the German, had succeeded in improving the sugar-beet seed so it was drought-resistant and could stand the strong Salinas Valley winds. Spreckels, the rich immigrant who had factories in the East as well as the West, promised to build the largest sugar refinery in the world on Buena Vista Rancho that had once belonged to old Juan Malarin. But this clever German refused to lay so much as a brick for the factory until farmers owning at least twenty-five thousand acres of land had contracted to plant their land in beets and to continue that contract over a period of five years! Money would pour in with beets at five dollars a ton. Beets were heavy. The factory would consume thirty-six hundred tons of beets a day, and in a season's run, turn out forty-five to sixty thousand tons of sugar. Spreckels and his sons had formed a company, and already had bought from the capitalist King thousands of acres of the old San Lorenzo that had once belonged to Benito's grandfather. They were even experimenting with an irrigation dam on the San Lorenzo where once the cattle of Feliciano Soberanes had roamed.

Spreckels were bringing in cheap labor too. Now, when the Chinese exclusion act cut off that source, the Japs were pouring into the valley to work in fields. Spreckels had a factory over the hill in the Pajaro Valley, so that on Jack's El Tucho land near Blanco the Chinese no longer needed for labor on the railroad were trying to head off the Japs and get work on beet contracts for the coming season in an effort to exist. The Japs had been paid a dollar seventy-five per ton for labor last year, but Chinese were so hard-hit they had brought down the price to from ninety cents to a dollar per ton. The editor of the *Owl*, that year of 1895, was writing editorials against the Japs and claimed they were like locusts swarming across the land and "God knows what will happen." But Japs were good workers and with the Chinese bidding against them for work a ranchero had a chance to make money. If only he, Benito Soberanes, could hold on to his inheritance of six hundred acres. Damn the bank where they made money so easy to borrow at twenty-four cents on the dollar and then took your land!

There *was* one way in which Benito could keep the land. Benito's wife was beautiful; the banker came to her and offered to wipe off the debt if she would be his mistress!

Doña Ada was proud and a descendant of the de la Guerras and W. E. P. Hartnell the trader. She refused.

"Then I hope someday you'll see your husband, Benito Soberanes, carrying his blankets on his back!" the angered banker told her.

The proud Spanish head went up and flashing eyes

looked at her opponent fearlessly. "He will be able to look people in the eye while he carries them," she said and closed the door.

But all was not ended then, for this banker was a power in the Salinas, and manager for the estate of Benito's father, Francisco Soberanes, and there was to be an auction to settle the estate and pay off the mortgages.

Benito and his wife, still on their own ranch, had borrowed a huge copper kettle that Francisco had bought for a yoke of oxen. The wash was boiling in this kettle when a representative of the banker came and demanded the kettle. Instead of waiting until Ada could remove the wash, he dumped it out onto the yellow soil of the rancho, put the kettle in a spring wagon, and went with it to the auction.

Benito was furious. He saddled his fastest horse and rode to the auction. He bid for the copper kettle against a junkman and it was knocked down for sixteen dollars. The next day the wash boiled merrily as ever.

When the mortgage was foreclosed and Benito and Ada drove away from their rancho forever, Francisco's great copper kettle went with them to a tiny cottage in Salinas City.

PART XII

For God, For Money, For Fraud! The Three Communistic Communities of Salinas Valley

For God

ASTRANGE procession of green and brown marched acre by acre up the Valley of the Salinas after Claus Spreckels built his $2,700,000 sugar factory on Buena Vista Rancho in 1897. He kept his promise to farmers. It *was* the largest refinery in the world, with all the latest equipment and acres of floor space that shot six stories up into the air.

SPRECKELS SUGAR MILL

Squat brown Japs with slant eyes labored to turn barley fields into rows of green beets, where once cattle of Estradas, Malarins, and Soberances had cropped pasture. Few families of the original grantees were left now, and tenant farmers often made as high as forty thousand dollars a year on shares on seven thousand acres! The old was gone forever, and these new people were beginning even to conquer the semi-arid land to the south of Salinas City, with dams and irrigation ditches.

There was little chance of watering the rolling hills of old Alberto Trescony's San Lucas Ranch far to the south, but in spite of drought and lawsuits over the old tinsmith's will irrigation prospered Julius Trescony and his brothers and sisters.

The cutting down of barley acreage made less competition for barley in the market, and Julius had learned through hard knocks how to manage dry farming by plowing at the right time to keep the moisture near the surface. And then Fortune smiled on this man who struggled valiantly against drought and lawyers' fees. San Lucas land was different! Barley raised there was a special type of hard barley that brewers in England clamored for. Trescony's barley from the Salinas was soon listed specially on the National Grain Market. It brought a premium and was shipped by the carload to London!

There was other news in the Trescony clan too, bad news from New York, where Rose's son, Leo Cristal, was a matinee idol on Broadway, charming the hearts of women in *The Parish Priest*. And there was the trouble. Leo was as generous as a child, a free spender of money that came from the San Lucas. He had married Margo, an artist's model, and had a child by her. Margo grew tired of Leo after a few months and went to court, which wrecked things at San Lucas, for Leo had to settle twenty thousand dollars on his daughter. It would take a good many carloads of Trescony barley to pay that off. The old tinsmith had erred in his will by one word, that precious twelve-letter word that meant success or hardship—"unencumbered"! Any of the legatees could borrow on his interest in the land, and *all* must suffer.

Charlie Romie, brother-in-law to David Jacks the moneylender, had started as a vaquero, but now he had taken over from the bank land of Mission Soledad lost by Benito Soberanes. There was great excitement in Salinas City. Charlie Romie had sold his six hundred acres to the Salvation Army!

"God's poor" were to be sent down from city slums to labor in the mission fields of Our Lady of Solitude where padres and Indians had sweated. These new folk were to use even the irrigation ditches surveyed and built by the missionary padres on the good rich land.

The "city people" were asked nothing but to work on the land for themselves until they had paid it off and could own it. Seed sheds and tools and equipment were provided by the Salvation Army Colony for all to use, and the "Army" built two-room shacks on the land before they arrived. Each plot was ten acres and sold for a hundred dollars an acre complete with shack.

At "Fort Romie" the stage was all set for the perfect proof of brotherly love and mutual prosperity, as one helped the other to gather God's bounty from the land.

In a big tent all could refresh their souls in prayer and song after the day's work was done.

But some Fort Romie people ran more to song and prayers than to work. "They planted things and set there expectin' God to do the rest! Some didn't even know what a cow was like or how to manage a hog that the 'Army' had presented to them. Besides, there wasn't no streets with shop windows to look at, and the 'Army' folks in charge kept tellin' you about thinkin' of the morrow and not usin' everythin' up as you went along. Why, that was all the excitement poor folks got out of life, a-wonderin' what was comin' in to eat the next day when you'd et everythin' up."

The majority of colonists were grateful and worked

hard on the fertile land. They had the new sensation of watching the seeds they planted send out shoots, flower, and bear food to eat, and a strange alchemy of hope and a new life took place within them. Some, who grew to love the song of the meadow lark and red-winged blackbird, took over land that had been given up by drones who had gone back where they could see shop windows.

Fort Romie became famous as a perfect communal experiment, and its fame spread to England where God's poor in London slums were a great problem to the British government that had once tried another way—Botany Bay prison ships.

One day word came that a "poet feller" Rudyard Kipling was on his way to Fort Romie. He was sent by the British to see the colony and talk to the people who lived in the free, open Salinas Valley! There were great doings on the land of Mission Soledad. The fine new "barracks" which had replaced the "meeting tent" was decorated for the occasion.

Rudyard Kipling was enchanted with the place. He stayed a week and was feasted off the land. He made a speech and told them all how fortunate they were to live in such a smiling valley of sunshine, instead of pea-soup fogs of London. Everybody in the colony had a chance to express what he thought about Fort Romie and its aims, so that Kipling could tell folks in England.

Just a few miles away, the moon looked down on the ruins of Our Lady of Solitude, where a padre now forgotten had starved to death for the sake of his Indian converts. And all through the valley were little settlements of brown-skinned men with slant eyes, who watched and worked in the beet fields by day and talked in their own language at night over rice and sake about the day when the many children they were now bringing into the world would own land in the Salinas. If Japanese couldn't own land, there was no law to stop *children* of Japanese born in America from owning land! Patience, quiet patience, and a silent mouth was all that was required among these people who labored in the fields of indifferent landholders.

MISSION SOLEDAD

2

For Money

ON A HIGH windy bench of land to the south, which had been granted in 1840 to a Mexican patriot for his active service against invading foreigners, a clever gringo lawyer made plans. He had taken half the grant as his fee for clearing a defective title and now the land was on his hands.

He had tried to sell to Spreckels, the sugar man, who had paid an option and then sent men in search of water for wells; not finding enough, he had let the option expire.

Now he would work another way. Colonies paid. Fort Romie thrived. Of course bottom land was rich and there was more water, but there would always be some soil-hungry ones who would come if land was cheap enough. People would settle his wind-swept acres if they didn't have to fight that howling wind alone. Most men liked neighbors to chat with, complain to, and sympathize with. He would make the land that old Californians called "Three Mile Flat" pay after all.

The lawyer went to San Francisco and talked fast about his great plan. A rich man from Peoria, Illinois, put up money and in no time surveyors were laying out small farms of the "California Home Extension Association" on land that had once belonged to an illiterate Spaniard.

Soon a little band of people, mostly victims of the

"Silver Campaign" panic, pitched tents on the windy Three Mile Flat of what old-timers in the valley called "no-good" land.

These poor strugglers paid twenty dollars an acre for their tiny patches. With high hope in their hearts they went to work building houses, in spite of occasional vaqueros who rode by and chided that "The wind'll blow the feathers off your chickens here at Arroyo Seco Rancho!"

There was no ease for these newcomers. Little calico-clad children with thin arms and pipestem legs lugged pails of water for home use from the one well until they cried from weariness. Women worked in the wind planting tiny patches of berries and raising turkeys and chickens, while the men built shacks, dug wells, and planted windbrakes of eucalyptus, which had just been introduced from the barren back country of Australia.

But the pieces were too small and the land too arid. One by one the little shacks grew more weather-beaten for lack of paint, either because their owners couldn't afford paint or because they were scrabbling so hard for a living that they had no time for "fancy" things like paint on a house. Contracts began to lapse, and land came back.

A man named Clarke put money into the venture and the California Home Extension became "Clarke's Colony." But that didn't change the way the wind blew or bring more water to the parched plateau where a scant livelihood must come from dry farming. The Salinas was winning the battle of Three Mile Flat.

After many of those disillusioned ones had left, clever Swiss and Americans searched once more for water—and found it! An irrigation system was put in with pumps and ditches that watered the plateau for only a dollar an acre for a whole year. Berries and onions and potatoes thrived now in spite of the Williwaws.

Prosperous Swiss bought up the land for five hundred

dollars an acre. Tiny ranches were thrown together. The colony was forgotten and the settlement on good-for-nothing Three Mile Flat became Greenfield, because dairymen could harvest four crops of alfalfa from the land in a year!

While Swiss at Greenfield milked their cows and watered alfalfa, and Danes threshed wheat and barley, and Japs harvested sugar beets in the Salinas, just over the hills at Jolon, a little band of Mexicans, Indians, and Spaniards prepared to honor Miguel Hidalgo the Liberator of Mexico as their grandfathers and fathers before them had done for ninety-eight years. Now Mexican Independence Day at the San Antonio Mission was all that remained as fiesta for these forgotten ones.

For days before the celebration, Spanish-speaking people streamed into the little settlement of Jolon. They came on horseback, most of them, with their fiesta clothing tied on behind the saddle. Bright-eyed old folks too feeble to ride came slowly over the rough roads in wagons.

Willow shelters were built along the creek where padres had come first, and fires were started. Soon the valley of the San Antonio was fragrant with the good smell of tamales and enchiladas cooking for the fiesta.

By afternoon of September 15th, the eve of Independence Day, all was ready. Toward sundown the band tuned up. Always the same players came: Trinidad Bojorques with his cornet, José Maria Carajal the fiddler, and Manuel Rojas the flutist.

First they played "The Star-Spangled Banner" as the American flag went slowly up the homemade flagpole. As it neared the top shouts of "Viva! Viva!" burst from the throats of those who had been conquered and were now forgotten in the rush of civilization. The Mexican flag followed Old Glory, and the little band played the "Himno Nacional"

of Mexico with more "Vivas" until you could scarce hear
Trinidad's cornet.

Then came the grand part, the explosions! Men had
worked all afternoon to make these fine explosions possible.
They had hauled blacksmiths' anvils over the rough mountain road in spring wagons, and piled one anvil on top of the
other, with a stick of dynamite underneath. They touched
these off one after the other. You could hear the explosions
for miles on Mexican Independence Eve. Perhaps even the
old priest Miguel Hidalgo, of Mexico, who had worked so
hard to free his people, could hear the explosion in heaven
and know that his good work was not forgotten in gringo
California!

Everyone was astir before dawn on Independence Day.
Horses' manes and tails were unbraided and brushed, and
their bodies rubbed with an oiled cloth to make them glisten.
The first rays of the sun picked up the shining polish of
saddles; martingales and bridles were eye-dazzling.

Children scrubbed within an inch of their lives were
dressed in bright calicoes, with ribbons in their hair that
were saved all year for the occasion. And the señoritas, aye
the señoritas in their best, casting eyes toward the young
caballeros in their spangled jackets and bright sashes! The
everthinning "old ones" were dressed in their decent black
silks. They all paraded slowly in a grand procession to the
Mission of San Antonio to hear the strange new Jesuit priest
from San Miguel say the Mass. For those with gray hair there
was sadness in the old ruins as they remembered the gay
days, the prosperous feast days, when the altar stood straight
and fine with many more tapers alight.

Then came the return procession and the barbecue.
Sometimes there were two whole steers, if it was a lucky
year and the rancheros around felt generous of heart. And
there were tortillas and empanadas, those delicious little fruit
pies that women made for days in preparation for fiesta.

Everything was free but the beer, and no one minded paying for the beer. Hadn't they saved up for months? They liked beer and it made the fights better.

Afterward there were games and races and cockfights. Young men with fine horses rode full tilt at rings on a pole, to hook them off with a lance. They swooped past roosters buried in the sand with their legs tied to a weight, and twisted the neck off. That was pescuza and everyone could not do it right, for the neck had to snap pronto and the head came off. Training for the pescuza was unfair, but young caballeros did train on the sly so that they could impress the señoritas, and after all, the horse had to know what it was all about.

The grand ball started at sundown, and lasted until sunrise when the arm of Carajal was numb from holding his fiddle box.

The last Mexican Independence Day at Jolon was over. Civilization in the Salinas had caught up and gone ahead of those who liked the old way better.

CATTLE BRANDS

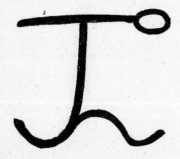

Feliciano Soberanes
SAN LORENZO

Carlos Espinosa
ARROYO SECO

3

Earthquake. 1906

BEDS SHOOK wildly in the dark of early morning! The earth rumbled along the Salinas. Spanish Californians and Mexicans knew what was happening, for the earth had trembled often before, but this was worse than most shocks and lasted longer. Terrified Italians, Portuguese, and Japanese, who had known earthquakes in their homeland, grabbed up children and made for the open, but to Danes and Swiss these earth-rocking shocks were a new thing.

Houses cracked and heavy tiles slipped from their moorings on roofs; dishes danced crazily on shelves and then crashed to the floor; brick chimneys fell all in a piece. There was great excitement in barnyard and pasture; cocks crowed, cattle bawled, and dogs howled. Another shock—and another! Then all was calm.

Except for the most pressing chores, there was little work done on farms and ranchos in the valley that 18th day of April. People wanted to talk to other people; to learn what had happened. They went to town.

Telegraph and telephone lines were down to the north and the south. Trains did not come through. Then the terrible news that San Francisco was ablaze!

Earthquake shocks had burst gas mains and the place was an inferno. Firemen and the military were blowing up whole blocks with dynamite in an effort to stop the terrible fire. Hundreds were homeless.

Brown, the butcher who had bought part of Atherton's Milpitas Rancho, was crazed with worry. His daughter was in San Francisco at school. No word. No way to get to her.

It was then that an old Spanish Californian reminded the gringo butcher of travel in the old days. "Take a horse and ride him until he's winded, patron; then borrow another until *he's* winded and *still* another and another until you finally come into the city. You will get there in twenty-four hours riding night and day. When gringos were coming, riders warning of trouble made it in twenty-four hours. You pick up and exchange on the way back until again you get your own horse and are home."

Brown started off, telephoning ahead as far as lines were up, for horses to be ready, then taking a chance to getting a horse. He found his daughter safe with other victims, huddled only in night clothes in Golden Gate Park.

The Browns brought back terrible stories. The whole town was burning; martial law to stop the looting; babies being born in the park with only blankets held up by women as a screen to keep new mothers from prying eyes. Doctors worked frantically taking care of the wounded, the terrified, who huddled in the smoke. Field kitchens were trying to feed the hungry.

"Pobrecitos, pobrecitos" (poor ones). Hearts of Spanish and Mexicans along the Salinas went out in pity and sympathy. They crossed themselves and murmured a prayer to ask the Blessed Mother to care for all these poor suffering gringos; then they went about gathering clothes and food to send.

Three days later when railroad tracks on the earthquake fault-line had been repaired, and a train came through, potatoes, flour, beef, mutton, and clothing went out of the Salinas Valley by the carload. Danes, Swiss, Portuguese, Basques, Italians, Americans, and French all shared with the homeless ones in the burning city.

The earthquake made a great change at the mouth of the Salinas and created a new industry. Polsena and Roleno de la Vierra, the Portuguese, had long ago joined their ancestors, but their nephews at the mouth of the river were prospering. They had a beautiful strawberry patch that brought in good money, for the berries were purchased by the grand new Del Monte Hotel that the Southern Pacific had built near Monterey.

Just after the earthquake, the de la Vierras irrigated their strawberries as usual, from the well they had put down. But the leaves began to curl. The plants died! The earthquake had opened up a seam and salt water had irrigated the berries.

Courageous de la Vierras again faced realities. They turned their strawberry fields into evaporating ponds, and soon the Salinas had its first and only commercial salt plant.

4

Waters of the Salinas Come Out of Hiding

Folks along the Salinas were scarce used to writing 1909 at the top of their letters, when news headlines screamed into the valley all the way from Monterey.

David Jacks, owner of a hundred thousand acres in the county, had died in the night! Jacks was *dead!*

It was a strange trick of fate that death should have taken the old land baron who was against irrigation, just as men discovered that the Salinas with its treacherous quicksands had lakes beneath its surface; lakes that would supply all the water needed for hundreds of thousands of acres of fertile land. Jacks would always shake his head over irrigation. "If God wanted the land of upper Salinas watered, why, he would have watered it" was always his answer to those who would adventure in the matter of water for the parched land.

But after all, on his rancho at Blanco near the river's mouth, Jacks had been getting as high as four hundred bushels of potatoes to the acre without water, and he shipped out as much as ten thousand tons annually. Why pay for pumping plants and ditches? And Danes dry-farming his Chualar and Los Coches places grew good crops with only rain to depend upon.

Jacks, who had been crafty with Spaniards and Mexicans and town governments alike over land, was dead! He couldn't take his land with him, even though he had boasted until the last that no one could enter the county of Monterey or leave it without spending most of his time on the land of David Jacks. Now, David Jacks dead was no better than the Indians who had worked in his fields for food alone, because of that horrible word "vagrant," or the Mexicans he had turned from their land.

Tongues clacked up and down the valley. Some said Jacks was good, remembering how he had fed the poor in drought years in Monterey, and that he had given a great sum of money to the Methodist College of the Pacific for a glass to observe the stars. Others, with resentment burning in them when they thought how he had taken their land, cursed his very soul. Now, who would get the land? How would it be divided between his children?

Then it was discovered that the canny Scot had once more outwitted the county. A year ago he had formed the David Jacks Corporation, a holding company which included all his children, and from which he drew only a hundred and fifty dollars monthly.

David Jacks was dead, and the papers were full of accounts of his success story. A special train was to run from Salinas City to Monterey to carry mourners.

Indians and Mexicans still remembering the things not printed, thought of the curse they had put upon Jacks that he would have no grandchildren, the curse that had persisted and brought results. Now they sat in little groups and cursed his very bones; some threatened to dig them up.

The man who had acquired so much land in life had not even a marker on the soil that covered him in death. Jacks dead was nameless.

By a strange trick of fate government men came to Benito Soberanes and his son Nat and asked these two, whose family had suffered at the hands of Jacks, to appraise the land in the valley of Salinas for the Jacks estate. "Be just," said they, "be fair to the Jacks Corporation and to your country."

And so it was that the brother and the nephew of Josefa Richardson took the papers and went over the old Scot's possessions. To be fair and just each did his work without consulting the other, then they compared results. There was only a difference of five dollars an acre. They split the difference and sent in the report that was used in court to determine the tax to be paid. All concerned felt that the appraisal was a fair and a just one.

The irrigation projects that David Jacks scorned now flourished! Tall, chimneylike vents stuck up all over the land to relieve pressure of this newly discovered underground water, and acres were flooded with liquid that brought gold into the hands of all who tilled fields in the Salinas.

Great tracts now went into sugar beets and the price of farms jumped with every pumping plant that was installed.

Beets ran twenty-two tons to the acre, and farmers received five dollars a ton. The Spreckels people offered every inducement possible to all who would plant the new blight-resistant beets. One million dollars had gone to farmers of Salinas in one year. With five thousand dollars a day paid out for labor, there was work in the great factory now for Spaniards and Mexicans who had been turned off their land.

For many at Fort Romie, the temptation was too much. They sold out, for eight or ten times what they had paid to the Salvation Army, to Swiss who fed dairy cattle on beet tops and sugary pulp from the great refinery. The barracks where prayers and song had been offered was turned into a general store.

A plant for evaporating milk went up only a few miles from the ruins of Mission Soledad; a factory with steaming chimneys, that gave work to a lot more people. Now Swiss could deliver their milk promptly with little expense. Alpine Lodge was built beside El Camino Real, where once a timid soul afraid of the wilderness had sowed mustard seed that explorers might find their way back to San Diego in the south. The big sign "Alpine Evaporated Milk" now told wayfarers where they were!

Danes and Swiss in their dairies were growing rich with the hidden water. Never again would drought be their enemy. They brought more of their countrymen over to share this prosperity in the valley. Some said that there were more people living in the Salinas from some towns in Denmark and Switzerland than were left behind.

These hard-working folk soon began to show their gratitude and loyalty to the country that had brought them security and happiness, and became American citizens. It was during one of these naturalization sessions that a Dane was asked by the judge:

"Are you a polygamist?"

Hanson shook his head doubtfully. "No, sir, but if I get to be a citizen, I'll be a Democrat."

Portuguese cattle men with rolling hillside lands, and Basques too, flourished. Irrigation brought beet pulp to fatten cattle quickly for market. These livestock people had seen hard days of drought, especially in 1898 when many herds had perished. Some had cut down even trees to feed animals the leaves in an effort to survive. Now they bought more cattle to feed and fatten on beet pulp. The cattle industry in the valley was increasing enormously. Irrigation and beet pulp made drought only a bad dream to forget as quickly as possible, for the "sugar campaign" came when feed on the hills was used up.

The Spreckels themselves, seeing the enormous profit in cattle raising, bought up more hillside land including Hartnell's Alisal, where they fed and fattened beef cattle on the by-products of their own factory. Hired men slept now in the dormitories of that first college in California, and they ate in the room where Hartnell's students had studied "morals and manners and essay-writing." Steers poked their heads through paneless windows of the ruined outside kitchen.

Spreckels ran a narrow-gauge railroad to the Alisal, on old trader Hartnell's place, for there was lime upon Gabilan Mountain where Captain Frémont had once hoisted Old Glory in defiance of Mexico. The Salinas had even provided the sons of a German immigrant with lime for their use in the manufacture of sugar.

The whiskered "Knights of the Road" began to look forward to their stay in the "jungle" of Salinas River willows on Estrada and Malarin land near the town of Spreckels, for there was champagne to be had near the sugar factory!

Cars of fermented beet pulp were often left on the siding for a number of hours until they could be moved. All that was necessary for a good drunk on the "capitalists" was to fill a couple of sacks with this pulp, carry it to the jungle, and squeeze it out into bottles. Then there was high-stepping among tramps, and part-singing—as many parts as men, most of them singing off key, when the potent "bubbly" from Salinas Valley took effect on them!

Bums planned their trips so that they could spend considerable time in the willow jungle of Buena Vista Rancho, while the sugar factory was working.

5

For Fraud.   1914

Now that the hard master drought had been sub-
jugated in the valley, that devil *water* turned up again in
full strength.

Rain poured down for days, bridges on the county road
were washed away, and the railroad bridge near Spreckels
had three spans missing before the first month of 1914 had
slipped into history. A thirty-five thousand dollar pumping
plant on old Esteban Munras's San Vicente washed out, and
acres of fertile bottom soil once more moved toward the sea.
The valley was a great muddy lake from top to mouth.
Beets, alfalfa, barley, and even usually arid acres that were
planted with an experimental crop of that rubber substi-
tute, guayule, were all underwater.

Twenty-five inches of rain fell in a short time, and
then as a climax to celebrate Washington's birthday there
was a cloudburst.

Eventually, the water would subside; there would be
heartaches, then men would plant and prosper again. But at
the top of the valley on Atascadero Rancho, where Estradas
had made fiesta and lost the land, heartaches and poverty
that would last for years were in the making.

A bankrupt eastern "promoter" had come fresh from
indictments for using the mails fraudulently. On borrowed
capital he paid down five hundred dollars and bought from

the Murphy Estate twenty-three thousand acres of Atascadero Rancho. He even bragged: "If I'd had a thousand
dollars I would have bought the country."

He had a precious thing, a "mailing list."

This clever one, E. G. Lewis, was to take from struggling clerks, widows, and old people, twenty-three million
dollars in ten years. The "Champion Borrower of All Times"
had arrived in the Salinas.

He sent telegraphic "appeals" east to those who could
believe no wrong of him in spite of what the Supreme Court
said, and within ninety days after the payment of that first
five hundred dollars he had raised and paid out a quarter of
a million dollars. Then Lewis limbered up his hypnotic
tongue on two hard-boiled bankers in San Francisco and
came away with a million dollars for which he had given
mortgage bonds on the land.

Men working on the railroad saw great oak trees, where
Estrada cattle had sheltered, blown up by dynamite to make
way for buildings of the new "Atascadero Colony." Lewis
bragged that the largest department store between San
Francisco and Los Angeles was to be put up. One hundred
and fifty men were employed in clearing off grounds to
make ready for the migration of "suckers" who would
purchase land, many of them with their life savings. The
old Atascadero adobe ranch house was demolished to make
way for a fine three-story colonnaded "Administration
Building," where business of "The Colony" would be trans-
acted. Foundations of a hotel went in.

On arid 2½-acre tracts, tiny switches of apple trees,
pears, and prunes were planted. Then, Lewis opened up his
gigantic campaign to sell land on the installment plan.

Beautiful broadsides filled with plans and pictures of
the proposed "colony" flooded the land. They went into the
homes of people who had been readers of the little news-
paper-print "home" magazine that Lewis had once pub-

lished. The magazine that rupture cures and electric "vitality belts for sexual troubles," and other fraudulent ads, had supported, but it had given the subscribers crochet patterns too. Now it gave them dreams of prosperity as well. There were pictures of grand esplanades at Atascadero Colony and the plans of a community cannery and evaporating plant which would be "owned" by the colonists and would buy up the crops and process them right on the colony's own grounds, keeping the profit for all who bought into the enterprise. There was to be a community printing press.

This promoter with the golden-tipped pen induced people to pull up stakes, to leave old friends and home, jobs and security, and come thousands of miles to invest their savings in a new business on so small a scale that they could not possibly make a living.

Lewis took from them not only their capital but their livelihood as well. He told them they could make a living on two and one half acres of dry land. The orchard would produce four hundred dollars a year per acre, together with vegetables and chickens. "One Acre, One Bee, and Liberty!"

Tired shopgirls, with dependent mothers and a longing to be free from stuffy stores and impatient customers, invested their savings and came; old people in the winterbound East, to whom California meant sunshine and ease, read the ad avidly and came with their lifetime savings to raise berries and chickens. Struggling office workers felt that at last a couple of acres of land of their very own were within their reach, and they cut loose forever from their desks.

Lewis sold them two and one half acres of land at eight hundred dollars an acre, when in reality it would take twenty-five or thirty acres of land at dry Atascadero for even an existence. Soon all the land was sold, and Lewis contracted to buy an additional rancho to the south of his holdings.

Then colonists ran out of money to keep going and

began to fail, orchards suffered from lack of water, and pumpkins for the dehydrating plant did not grow. Disillusioned ones began to complain.

Lewis had to do something. This son of an Episcopal minister was a charming man and a convincing talker. He wanted all to prosper and live happily. In spite of what they had gone through, many of his followers still loved him and remained loyal. To those faithful ones who were struggling on he offered a new chance to recoup their money by "wildcatting" for oil, if they would invest a dollar a month. There was millions to be made in oil!

The poor came through handsomely on that bait. Lewis then put up Atascadero land he had contracted for, as security on a mortgage, and no one even asked questions.

In four years, Lewis the champion borrower tossed six million dollars of his followers' money into dry holes of various sorts, and sold his sucker list to raise more money. Then he went into bankruptcy again.

Plaster fell off the tall gracefully columned Administration Building, and machinery rusted in the dehydrating plant. Receivers were appointed for "Atascadero Estates" and a San Francisco bank was about to foreclose on the mortgage that Lewis had given on the colony, which left the landholders holding the sack. Tiny farms were deserted when some could hang on no longer, but there remained a faithful few who still believed in the hard-luck stories of their hero Lewis, when he told them that the government was persecuting him. They still sent him driblets of money.

In reply to an "appeal" to the loyal, one man wrote after ten years of struggle:

Dear Mr. Lewis: Happy New Year to you and Yours. Forwarded this day a check for ———— dollars to the bank for you, and only wish I could send more as I am sorely pressed for funds. *Fight the scoundrels to the limit.* Again wishing you good luck and success, I remain yours,   Loyally

In a note to the treasurer of Lewis Credits Committee, another wrote:

Thank God I am not a parasite, at least not yet against E. G. Lewis. I have loaned several hundred dollars and am sorry it was not more.

The "scoundrels" closed in. Then Lewis the martyr got more than half the creditors to turn over their real estate receipts and their cash payments into his "Reconstruction Fund." This he used for mining. He had a shallow producing well by that time and he sent a little money for a "sweetener" to those who had contributed with cash but no real estate coupons, but only a trifle of what they had given him.

The bankers in San Francisco took over and Lewis the great promoter landed in the penitentiary, because the editor of *Sunset Magazine,* now a great power in California, took up the torch for the poor strugglers, made an investigation, and aired thoroughly the frauds of the "Champion Borrower of All Times."

Trees at Atascadero Colony went unpruned and died for lack of water. Roofs of little homes began to sag. Clerks went back to desks, and old people died brokenhearted. A boys' school rented the buildings; only a few colonists were left to struggle on against debt and drought!

6

Fame

WHILE THE Salinas was bringing disappointment and disillusionment to the strugglers at Atascadero, just a few miles to the north downriver at Paso Robles (pass of oaks) Ignace Paderewski, up to his neck in the warm comfort of mud, was bringing fame to the Salinas.

A few days before, the Polish pianist had arrived in San Francisco suffering frightfully at the hands of his old enemy neuritis. Concerts were canceled. The Steinway man went for a doctor, but before the doctor arrived an old friend of Paderewski's came to see him, Sir Henry Heymann, the musician.

"There is no use calling a doctor," Sir Henry told the pianist, "because a doctor cannot cure you immediately and that's what you want. But there *is* something else for you to do. You must go to Paso Robles and take the mud baths there, for your arm. They are magical—so many of my friends have been cured, and I am also enjoying the treatment myself because I, too, have neuritis badly. It is almost infallible, that treatment at Paso Robles."

And so it was that a mudhole on the Salinas, which long ago padres had discovered when they saw a bear wallowing, drew the suffering Pole into its warm brown comfort and cured him as no European spa had been able to do!

"The cure was miraculous," Paderewski says in his

memoirs. "After three weeks of treatment I continued my tour and finished it in comfort."

The Salinas had wooed and won the eternal gratitude of the famous musician-statesman with her mud. Before he left he had purchased a great rancho of his own, not far away. He sent to his estate in Switzerland for one of his countrymen to come and run the new rancho. He developed his lands and planted hundreds of acres of almonds and prunes, and a vineyard which was a great success, because the Swiss-Italian colonists near-by bought the grapes to make their own wine. San Ignacio, the dream ranch of Ignace Paderewski the Pole, was a reality in the Salinas.

There were great doings, too, in the county seat, where folks were making ready to welcome a home-town boy. Frank Bacon, the photographer turned actor years before, was returning famous at seventy. The play Frank had written long ago in his little studio between "sitters" was called *Lightin'* and had been running for years in the east. "Play-acting" paid!

Frank hadn't changed with fame or the passing of years. He was a bit upset that now the place was called only Salinas, instead of Salinas City, but he enjoyed seeing old friends who once shrugged shoulders and tapped foreheads when they talked about him. He liked the good meal they got up for him, and he made a speech.

"When you find out what you want to do, go do it. I pretty nearly didn't, and I wouldn't be getting a good feed and all this 'home town boy makes good' stuff now. If *you* go early enough you can have more chicken dinners with canned peas and mashed potatoes given for *you*."

Leo Cristal, that other matinee idol, was back in the valley too, but fame had forgotten him, a "down and outer," still delightful and generous. He had borrowed on his interest of the land at San Lucas until there was no more, no granddad now to fall back on.

In his frayed and ragged rodeo shirt with the Tularcitos Rancho brand embroidered on it, he came to see the new baby born to his cousin Julius Trescony II, who now lived in old Alberto's adobe. He brought the young mother a box of candy purchased with borrowed money. He was gay and made her laugh, this gentle, generous don. He was waiting for a new part. A *grand* new part that would bring him fame.

But the grandson of old Alberto Trescony, the tin-smith, was never again to hear the shouts and clapping of an audience. Just as the fine new part materialized, Leo heard of another actor down and out, and ill, in a boardinghouse in San Francisco, and went to see him. The day was wet, and Leo, rain-soaked, took pneumonia. When he breathed his last, the man who ran the little Basque hotel in San Francisco was sad, not because Leo owed him two hundred dollars, but because he had lost a friend. "If he had owed me twice as much, I would still love him!"

Future fame for the fertile valley was walking around the streets of Salinas in the form of a gangling high-school boy who dreamed dreams of being a writer; a boy with the soul of a perfectionist in the matter of words, and an insatiable curiosity about his fellow men and the workings of their minds, hands, and hearts.

There were plenty of hard struggles ahead for this Salinas-born son of the county treasurer, this apostle of the "blood, guts, and bastard" school of novelists, but eventually young John Steinbeck was to shake the whole of America with his crusading *Grapes of Wrath*.

Far away in New York fame smiled on a boy from the mouth of the Salinas. Carlos Vierra, the hard-working nephew of the Portuguese Polsena and Roleno de la Vierra, was hailed by art critics of the effete East, as "a master painter of his time."

While Salinas folk swelled with pride over their own

who had gained recognition, a man famed in another way was dreaming of his empire to come, and quietly buying up land in San Antonio Valley near Jolon, which was to be the nucleus of that empire. This man had great power and influence. He could do much to bring on war or to affect the peace of nations, through his daily columns in black and white. One day he would control whole communities in the Salinas and her tributaries, and build a castle. William Randolph Hearst now owned land where padres and Indians had built ditches and labored in the fields and chanted their Canticle to the Dawn.

At Los Coches, the deeds of that famous land baron David Jacks were living after him. The Jacks Corporation had a buyer for Los Coches, that Jacks had bought at a sheriff's sale fifty years before, but the title was not clear.

The Jacks Corporation informed the heirs of Josefa Richardson that they still had an interest in the land, and that the Jacks Corporation was willing and ready to enter into negotiations with them to acquire deeds from them.

The offer of ten thousand dollars was made and grabbed up eagerly by the heirs of old Josefa. Each received twenty-five hundred dollars from the Jacks Corporation on a compromise pending the negotiation for the delivery of the deeds by the Richardsons to the Jacks.

Then it developed that there were minor children involved! Negotiations were suspended, and steps taken to have a guardian appointed to represent the minors' interest. But the guardianship was made in San Francisco at the suggestion of the Jacks Corporation and *paid for by them.* As far as it is known, no appraisers were appointed by any court to appraise the minors' interest, but nothing was done by the Richardsons who took their money and were thankful, for even if things were wrong they had no money to fight a great and powerful corporation. They didn't even look into the matter of *why* the Jacks Corporation was willing to pay them ten thousand dollars to clear the title on land worth a million dollars, after being in possession of the property for fifty years, when a quiet title would have been cheaper and quicker!

It was not until many years later that a possible explanation of that title flaw came to light. The sheriff's sale of Josefa's land had been conducted by the constable instead of the sheriff; but the sheriff gave the deed, making the transaction illegal!

PART XIII

Green Gold and Trouble

I

Lettuce. 1921

O N "BOTTOM LAND" of Blanco district, which Rafael Estrada had sold with tongue in cheek to the "Democratical Hypocritical Secessionist" James Bardin, there was prosperity. Beans and beets grew well and brought in plenty. The namesake son of that first James, who had come from Mississippi with his family and two black slaves, was a man of standing in the valley. He and his brothers had bought more land to add to the holdings left by their father, and "Jim" Bardin's name was on a new hospital in Salinas. Indeed, the Bardins were doing well; they now owned the fine Rancho Alisal so beloved by Hartnell, and their hired hands lived in the adobe halls of learning. But prosperity didn't stop Bardin ambition.

In a smaller valley to the north some farmers found they could grow lettuce that would ship well and bring fancy prices in eastern markets. Lettuce shippers sent their agents into the Salinas in search of landowners who would devote acres to the planting of this new crop.

Most farmers, satisfied with a good income from beets and beans, refused to experiment, but that year of 1921 the Bardins, the Vierras, and a few neighbors planted little patches of lettuce on their rich flood-washed bottom land.

The heads were huge! The crop ran four hundred crates to the acre!

Soon a crop of sixty-eight carloads was packed for shipment in a shed at Castro's village of Del Monte Junction, and started on its experimental journey to the New York market. At Blanco a little group of ambitious farmers waited, their hopes high.

The lettuce shipped perfectly. Easterners went wild over these giant solid heads of lettuce from the Valley of the Salinas. A new era of prosperity started with the popularization of vitamins!

But there were troubles aplenty. Inexperience in growing and handling, and fog and wind, made crop failures and heavy hearts. Sometimes, in those first years, the entire crop was lost, but the courageous ones pushed on, working and experimenting, until once more they had outwitted the handicap nature had given them. Finally a strain of lettuce was developed that would resist cold fogs and wind of the Salinas.

Lettuce began to nose out sugar beets and beans as a major crop near the river's mouth, and it was a strange trick of Fate on the Bardins that the "good-for-nothing" thirty acres of flood land old James had "thrown in" for his buyer to pay taxes on brought the highest yield in the vicinity. It was priceless now!

In less than ten years that pathetic first shipment of sixty-eight cars swelled to twenty thousand cars a year, with three growing seasons to bank on. Men became rich beyond belief in one year or they lost everything and had to borrow when an untimely rain came. Green gold was gambler's fare, but there were plenty to gamble for such high stakes.

Huge icing plants were built in what had once been Deacon Howe's mustard field. Extra tracks were laid, and special refrigerator cars built.

A cry went up for farm labor, for "stoop crop" workers. The Salinas would hire all comers with strong backs and willing hands, to weed, cultivate, and pack her gold for market. Filipinos came with gamecocks under their arms, to work alongside of Mexicans and Japs, but still there were not enough hands. Agents went to the drought-ridden Middle West "dust bowl" in search of laborers.

In 1931 there were fifty-eight thousand acres of green gold growing in the Valley of the Salinas, on land once owned by Estradas, Malarins, Spences, Soberanes, Hartnells, and Castros; on land where the lost Portola had camped when he searched for Monterey Bay and on land where the feet of Frémont's men had raced through the mustard to escape the lassos of angry Spanish California patriots.

2

Major Dwight D. Eisenhower Reports. 1930

LONG BEFORE lettuce experiments started near the river's mouth, scientists were working on a practicable commercial method for growing and extracting rubber from the guayule shrub up in the drier parts of the Salinas valley.

Early in the century when the advent of the automobile made rubber a necessity and plantation rubber was just coming into being, the Dutch-controlled Intercontinental Rubber Company saw the advantage of having rubber nearer at hand than the Far East. This company's experts explored the field and discovered guayule in Mexico, where natives extracted the rubber for their playing balls by chewing the little shrub. One great advantage in this plant was the fact that it produced rubber when grown on arid land not good for anything else.

The company promptly set about growing and experimenting with guayule for commercial purposes both in Mexico and in California, and early in 1930 the stage was set. The company had 1,988 acres of guayule growing in the upper Salinas Valley and 6,542 in California. At their experimental station near the town of Salinas, they had for nineteen years carried on exhaustive research.

In April, 1930, the results of this research were made

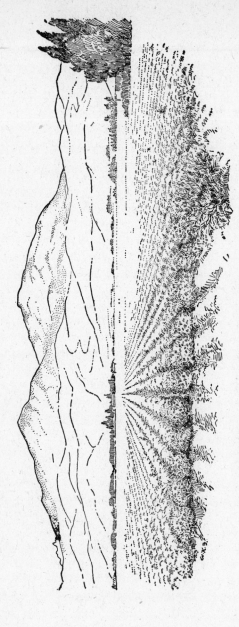

GUAYULE PLANTATION NEAR GREENFIELD

public by Dr. D. Spence, vice-president in charge of research and development of the Intercontinental Rubber Company, and international authority on rubber, in a paper published in the *Journal of the American Chemical Society*, entitled "Cultivation and Preparation of Rubber in the United States." He pointed out that the United States imported from the Far East practically all the raw rubber it consumed, which then was a billion pounds a year. If for *any* reason this supply was cut off, or its output curtailed, the far-reaching consequences in America could easily be estimated. Guayule grown within the borders of the United States was the answer to this serious problem.

Then the Intercontinental Rubber Company informed the United States War Department of this possibility of growing rubber in the United States, and invited government officials to inspect the company's thousands of acres of guayule and their experimental station near Salinas.

Accordingly, Major Van B. Wilkes of the Engineers Corps and Major Dwight D. Eisenhower of the Infantry arrived to inspect and report the rubber doings along the Salinas.

Dr. David Spence and Dr. McCallum (who had originally smuggled the guayule seeds into the United States from Mexico in a tobacco pouch and had worked for years on the project) took the War Department investigators through the plant and explained all in detail. They pointed out with figures the grave possibility that if a war should come and ships from the Far East were unable to deliver rubber, procurement under the present conditions would be impossible, and this would seriously handicap the country. They gave Major Eisenhower and Major Wilkes a brief history of the guayule rubber industry and the methods of extracting the eleven to fifteen per cent of rubber that the shrub contained, and told them that several companies were ready to furnish the finished product to consumers. They showed fields of the gray low-growing guayule in the Salinas, and pointed out the fact that in many states on poor land, small grain and even cotton planting could be reduced in favor of guayule which without water would produce the much-needed rubber for which the United States was now wholly dependent upon an overseas supply. This would enable the United States to build up a rubber supply for use in an emergency.

There was another important factor in the production of guayule that was not forgotten. After the first planting of seed and weeding, most of the work could be done by mechanical means—something to consider in a country which must compete with the low-cost human labor of the Far East. This made the cost of producing guayule rubber and delivering it to New York no greater than for the same amount of imported hevea rubber. Guayule cultivation would give employment to thousands of American farmers, laborers, and mechanics on land that was good for little else, instead of sending some two to three hundred millions of dollars out of the country each year to pay for imported rubber.

Then the company opened their files and showed the military men a table with the exact poundage production:

First year 300 to 400 pounds per acre.

Third year 1,000 to 1,200 pounds per acre.

Fourth year 1,400 to 1,600 pounds per acre.

Ninth year 2,200 to 2,900 pounds per acre.

In 1927 the Intercontinental Rubber Company had introduced a superior grade of rubber known as Ampar for which a premium of one and one-half cents per pound was paid, and Thomas Edison stated in a letter to the company that he had tested another set of guayule tires for fourteen thousand miles and they still appeared perfectly sound in all respects.

There was no doubt but that guayule was the answer

BRANCH OF GUAYULE PLANT
AND, ABOVE RIGHT, FLORETS
ENLARGED

for the United States, now almost entirely dependent upon overseas sources for its rubber. But to succeed this project must have the government back of it as had many other ventures in agriculture.

All these facts were incorporated in a report to the War Department that Major Eisenhower made in June of 1930. The report was beautifully written up, typed and handed in —and nothing more was heard from it.

The Salinas was used to shelved reports. Hadn't Malaspina's report to Spain on why the new province of Alta California did not prosper been shelved, and the writer of it been banished from his homeland? There was always politics in high places to consider, "old ones" along the river reminded these young ones with high hopes. Besides, the lettuce was creeping fast along the valley, for increased money made more pumping plants possible.

A few ranchers held on with their rows of gray fuzzy low-growing guayule—and then the rubber plant went down to defeat in its fight against politics and green gold. Acre by acre it was grubbed up and burned.

3

Riots

Asteady stream of dust-powdered rickety mechanical wrecks, piled high with household goods and spew-
ing children at every stop, labored over the grade once
trecked by padres and explorers seeking the new land of
promise.

The "Okies" had come!

When cars broke down and were forced to stop by the
roadside, half-naked little children with pinched faces and
eyes too old, grabbed eagerly for the unsprayed nubbins still
hanging to trees in neglected orchards of Atascadero Colony.
As the travelers moved on down the valley past San Miguel
Mission, where Franciscan fathers labored once more under
the protection of Esteban Munras's All-Seeing Eye, and
toward the thriving town of King City, the drought-glazed
eyes of grownups brightened. Here were *thousands* of acres
of beans being dusted with insecticide by planes that
whirred overhead.

Then came the green of beets, tilled by little brown
men with slant eyes, and *miles* of light-green lettuce, where
blue-shirted crews labored in the wind to load great trucks.
At every ranch gate there was a sign out for help. California!
Land of work and plenty!

Sixty-five thousand acres of lettuce were waiting for
their backs and hands to help in the harvest. "Little Okla-

homas" sprang up all along the valley, where these newcomers huddled together in makeshift shacks or "company
houses." Prosperity was on for "dust bowlers."

Before long trouble started brewing. Each year when
harassed growers watched weather forecasts with fear in
their hearts lest a rain come a day early and split open the
tight heads before they could be harvested, agitators went
out into fields to talk laborers into striking for more pay.

"They *have* to give it to you," was the cry up and down
the valley. "You got 'em where the hair's thin. If the crop
isn't harvested quick they lose it and all they got invested.
We got these big guys by the neck."

For a few years, growers, gambling against rain and
the overlapping of lettuce crops with those in the Imperial
Valley which would break the market, gave in. Anything to
save the crops!

Then in 1936 growers banded together and decided
they had been squeezed dry enough. They refused the raise.

War was on. Riots broke out in the streets of Salinas
and headlines blazed across the nation. Men hit each other
over the head with ax handles. Carpenters working on buildings tossed chunks of two-by-four to friends down in the
milling mass of rioters. Okies put razor blades inside potatoes and threw them at grower's cars. Special police came.

Bewildered, the grandsons and great-grandsons of those
who had come first watched the bloodshed once more in the
Salinas. There was Robert Malarin the tinner, son of Urbano
and grandson of old Juan Malarin the Peruvian, who worked
in a hardware store and saw men buying ax handles to use as
bludgeons, and Ulderico Hartnell, musician grandson of the
Lancashire trader. Benito Soberanes, grandson of old Feliciano, watched from the door of his little real estate office,
and with him *his* son, a sugar boiler at Spreckels. All these
people whose ancestors had owned and lost the land watched
Danes and Swiss and Portuguese and Basques and Italians

and their sons, who owned it now, fight new people who had come to harvest crops!

The newspaper *American Citizen* of San Francisco on September 26, 1936, was full of the lettuce strike that had gone on now for four weeks while lettuce rotted or went to seed in the fields. It talked of the terrible riots and bloodshed over the "closed shop" which was just used as an excuse to put growers on the spot. The skeleton of "preferential hiring" was rattled. The *American Citizen* claimed that an ex-convict Red was the chief Salinas agitator.

The strike went on and rioting grew worse day by day.

Then the people of Salinas were warned of a Communist advance heading toward town. The way they intended to come was all marked out. Those who warned brought red flags they had found, to prove their point! Airplanes were sent to reconnoiter, and ranchers got ready to defend their property against Communists!

Soon, angry red-faced Highway Department men roared into Salinas. They cursed all over the place. "What blankety-blank fool had taken all the red danger signals that they had put up along the road where they intended to work?"

Finally growers and laborers came to agreement. Another wave of bloodshed had washed over Salinas soil and passed into history. But in a short time young men from all over America were to come to the Salinas and prepare themselves to shed blood all over the world.

4

Rumors of War

T HE WAR in Europe was creeping ever closer to the Salinas. Government men swarmed into the valley to buy up thousands of acres to be used for the training of troops. The even climate made an ideal training ground.

Great Fort Ord was started near the sea, on part of the land owned by the grandchildren of Esteban Munras, and by Bardins, and the Jacks Corporation; a flying school at King City on the land of Feliciano Soberanes' San Lorenzo. William Randolph Hearst had to let go a hundred fifty thousand acres of his empire in Jolon Valley for Camp Hunter Liggett, named after Lieutenant General Hunter Liggett who had the distinction of leading the greatest number of tactical fighting men ever to be assembled in the history of the world, during the Meuse-Argonne offensive. Barracks went up on low hills overlooking the peaceful ruined Mission San Antonio where Junípero Serra had first raised the cross. Military roads pushed through wild hills where padres had traveled grizzly-infested trails. Milpitas, Los Ojitos, and El Piojo ranchos all went to war! Deer and quail were startled by rifle practice and thundering trucks, and magpies scolded in vain over the state of affairs.

Between Old Estrada's Atascadero land and the mud springs of Paso Robles, building started on Camp Roberts. A flying field for army pilots was made at San Lucas in the barley fields once so beloved by old Alberto Trescony the tinsmith!

Little brown men with slant eyes worked on in the lettuce and beets, and watched guns and tanks and heavy machinery roar by on rail and on the roads. They saw sons of Danes and Swiss, and Portuguese and Italians, leave the farms for military camps.

The whole Salinas Valley was soon flooded. This time with young men in khaki who had come from all over America to learn in the Salinas how to kill other men.

PART XIV

Trucks in the Silent Night

T HE DAY was clear and hills were golden. Cars filled
with laughing girls and soldiers on leave sped along the valley. Lettuce fields were bathed in Sabbath quiet, and in farmhouses men rested weary muscles in preparation for the week
to come, while they read comic sheets or listened to the radio.
Women "washed up" after the Sunday dinner.

Soldiers with girls on their arms jostled one another on
crowded streets of towns, and movie ticket-takers prepared
for the afternoon rush. High-school boys in Sunday best
kidded on street corners.

Then in cafés, farmhouses, cocktail bars, hotels, and
camps, news blared from thousands of radios:

"The Japs! Pearl Harbor bombed!"

There was a sudden hush as men gasped with horror; then came activity such as the valley had never known before.

Streets were suddenly emptied. Soldiers headed for camps, and farmers and businessmen rushed with guns to stand guard over electric plants and telephone exchanges and water supplies, lest the little slant-eyed men who had worked in their fields destroy them. Frightened Okies turned tail on bean field and lettuce patch, packed jallopies with children and possessions, and headed east.

By sunset, officers had found guns and a Japanese lieutenant's uniform in the house of a Jap who had been "so kind and thoughtful and always remembered birthdays of American children."

Dusk came, but no lights twinkled in the Salinas that night of December 7th.

Then in the dark, army trucks began to roll along the valley past the great silent sugar factory, the beet fields, and lettuce and beans. All night they passed, shaking the very earth as they rumbled by San Miguel where Franciscans prayed at the altar just under Esteban Munras's All-Seeing Eye.

On they traveled, past the healing mud of Paso Robles and the scraggly orchards of Atascadero, past Santa Margarita where once padres had stored grain in case of famine.

Up the mountain from a darkened silent Salinas Valley they went, these trucks loaded with grandsons and great-grandsons of those the valley had prospered: Spaniards, Mexicans, Peruvians, Basques, English, Scotch, Danes, Swiss and Portuguese—Americans all—riding through the night with other boys from other valleys all over America, on almost the very trail once trod by padres; out of the valley, to fight for their right to till the soil of the Salinas.

Rains came and washed away their footprints.

"The river's up!"

Acknowledgments

WITHOUT the hands and hearts and heads of a great many people, this book could not have been written. Special gratitude is due to members of old Spanish California and early American families along the Salinas who gave freely of their time, and the opportunity to examine old documents and manuscripts. To them the writer owes the loan of old family portraits which were copied in pen and ink.

Without the patience and hard work of Miss Thorne in the Monterey County Clerk's office, and her great help in copying legal documents and records there would be sad lapses in the continuity. Special thanks, too, should be given Miss Ellen Frink of the Monterey County Free Library for her help in tracking down old books and newspaper files; to Mrs. Bertha Hellum and her library staff in Monterey, and the staff of the Pacific Grove Public Library, as well as Miss Mabel Gillis of the California State Library. There is deep appreciation in the heart of this writer to Miss Alice Griffin of San Lucas who helped to clear up many difficulties and who so generously allowed the reproduction of her famous collection of old cattle brands, and to Lady Maria Antonia Field for the quaint old map of San Vicente Rancho.

Mr. Vivian of the King City *Rustler* and his staff were most helpful as was the Franciscan, Father Thaddeus of Mission San Miguel, and Mrs. Mary Green, custodian of Monterey Customs House Museum.

No effort was made to include all the people of the Salinas Valley who helped to make its history. In such a book as this there must be, as in the iceberg, far more than appears on the surface.

It seems fitting to close with the words of Padre Francisco Palou, one of the earliest historians of California:

"I am aware that neither Homer among the poets, nor Demosthenes among the orators, neither Aristotle nor Solon among the sages failed to err, because although they were eminent sages, orators and poets, they were always men. The misery of our nature is great; and while those that write do not cease to be men, there will always be men who observe them. Remember thine own frailty, and thou wilt have compassion on mine."

Bibliography

ABBOTT, CARLISLE, *Recollections of a California Pioneer*. New York: Neale Publishing Co., 1917.

ADAMS, E. D., "English Interest in the Annexation of California," *American Historical Review*, July, 1909, p. 744-763.

ALDEN, ROLAND H., and IFFT, JOHN D., *Early Naturalists in the Far West*. San Francisco: California Academy of Sciences, 1943.

ATHERTON, GERTRUDE, *Adventures of a Novelist*. New York: Liveright, Inc., 1932.

ATKINSON, F. M. *One Hundred Years in the Pajaro Valley, 1769-1868*. Watsonville: Register and Pajaronian Print, 1934.

BANCROFT, HUBERT HOWE, *History of California*. San Francisco: History Co. Publishers, 1888.

Bay of San Francisco, A History. Chicago: Lewis Publishing Co., 1892.

BOLTON, HERBERT EUGENE, *Anza's California Expedition* (5 vols.). Berkeley: University of California Press, 1930.

BRYANT, EDWIN, *What I Saw in California, 1846*. Santa Ana: Five Arts Press, 1936.

BURNS, WALTER NOBLE, *The Robin Hood of Eldorado*. New York: Coward McCann, 1932.

CHAPMAN, CHARLES E., *A History of California: The Spanish Period*. New York: The Macmillan Co., 1921.

CHASE, J. SMEATON, *California Coast Trails*. Boston and New York: Houghton Mifflin Co., 1913.

CLELAND, ROBERT GLASS, *A History of California: The American Period*. New York: The Macmillan Co. 1922.

"Crimes and Careers of Tiburcio Vasquez," *Evening Free Lance Press*, Hollister. 1927.

DAVIS, WM. HEATH, *Seventy-five Years in California* (a reissue and enlarged, illustrated edition of *Sixty Years in California*) Edited by Douglas S. Watson. San Francisco: John Howell, 1929.

DRURY, AUBREY, *California, an Intimate Guide*. New York: Harper and Brothers, 1935.

ELDER, DAVID PAUL, *The Old Spanish Missions of California*. San Francisco: Paul Elder Co., 1913.

ELDRIDGE, ZOETH SKINNER, *History of Monterey County*. San Francisco: Elliot and Moore, 1881.

ENGELHARDT, ZEPHYRIN, *Missionaries of California*. San Francisco: James H. Bang Co., 1908.

——— *Mission Nuestra Señora de la Soledad*. Santa Barbara: Mission Santa Barbara, 1929.

——— *San Antonio de Padua, The Mission in the Sierra*. Santa Barbara, 1929.

FIELD MARIA ANTONIA, *California Speaking*. Privately printed, 1934.

GUINN, JAMES MILLER, *History and Biographical Record of Monterey and San Benito Counties*. Los Angeles: Historic Record Co., 1910.

Harrison Series of Pacific Coast, Pamphlet 3. San Francisco: Pacific Press, 1889.

HITTELL, THEODORE H., *The Adventures of James Capen Adams, Mountaineer and Grizzly Bear Hunter of California*. Boston: Crosby, Nichols, Lee and Co.; San Francisco: 117 Washington St., 1861. Reprinted, New York: Charles Scribner's Sons, 1911.

HOOVER, MILDRED BROOKE, *Historic Spots in California. Counties of the Coast Range*. Stanford Press, 1937.

HUNT, ROCKWELL D., and NELLIE VAN DE GRIFT SANCHEZ,

A Short History of California. New York: Thomas Y. Crowell Co., 1929.

JAMES, GEORGE WHARTON, *Heroes of California. In and Out of the Old Missions of California.* Boston: Little, Brown and Co., 1916.

JOCHMUS, A. C., *The City of Monterey, Its People, Its Connection with the World, Anecdotes, Legends, Romances, Achievements, 1542-1930.* Pacific Grove, Calif.: Privately published, 1930.

MASON, J. ALDEN, *The Ethnology of Salinean Indians.* Berkeley: University of California Press, 1912.

PADEREWSKI, IGNACE JAN, and LAWTON, MARY, *The Paderewski Memoirs.* New York: Charles Scribner and Sons, 1938.

PALOU, FRANCISCO, *Historical Memoirs of New California.* Translated into English from the manuscript in the archives of Mexico; edited by Herbert Eugene Bolton. Berkeley: University of California Press, 1926.

REED, RALPH D., *Geology of California.* Tulsa, Okla.: American Association of Petroleum Geologists, 1933.

ROBINSON, ALFRED, *Life in California Before the Conquest.* San Francisco: Privately printed by J. T. Russell, 1925.

SANCHEZ, NELLIE VAN DE GRIFT, *California Place Names. Their Meaning and Their Romance.* San Francisco: A. M. Robertson, 1914.

———— *Spanish Arcadia.* Los Angeles: Powell Publishing Co., 1929.

SAUNDERS, CHARLES FRANCIS, and CHASE, J. SMEATON, *The California Padres and Their Missions.* Boston: Houghton Mifflin, 1915.

SMITH, FRANCES RAND, *The Mission of San Antonio de Padua.* Stanford University Press, 1932.

SPENCE, D., "Cultivation and Preparation of Rubber in the United States," *Industrial and Engineering Chemistry,* April, 1930, p. 384.

WATKINS, MAJOR ROLIN C., *History of Monterey and Santa Cruz Counties*. Chicago: S. J. Clarke Publishing Co., 1925.

WOEHLKE, WALTER V., "E. G. Lewis. The Champion Borrower of All," *Sunset Magazine*, May, September, October, November, December, 1925, January, 1926.

Note by the Illustrator

I AM GREATLY beholden to the following persons and institutions for material: Mr. B. A. Soberanes and Mr. N. Soberanes of Salinas; Mrs. Paul Soberanes of Oakland; Lady Maria Antonia Field; Father Thaddeus of Mission San Miguel; Mrs. Elsie Martinez and Miss Harriet Dean of Carmel; Mr. Julius Trescony of Rancho San Lucas; Prof. F. M. MacFarland of Stanford University; the Pacific Grove Museum; the Guayule Rubber Emergency Project, Salinas.

It was greatly desired to include portraits of Esteban Munras and Alberto Trescony but apparently no likenesses are extant.

The portrait of the California Vulture, or Condor, is a pen and ink rendering of a wash drawing given me in 1903 by the late Louis Agassiz Fuertes, one of America's greatest delineators of birds.

"Grizzly Adams and Ben Franklin" is a copy of a woodcut published in 1861 in Theodore H. Hittell's "The Adventures of James Capen Adams, Mountaineer and Grizzly Bear Hunter, of California" (Boston: Crosby, Nichols, Lee and Company. Reprinted by Charles Scribner's Sons, 1911). The original drawing was by Charles Nahl, a well known and gifted artist who probably made sketches from life. The late Judge Hittell related to me the circumstances which led him to write the life of Adams. The latter had brought his animals, including two tame grizzlies (Ben Franklin and Lady Washington) to San Francisco and Mr.

Hittell, then a newspaper reporter, was detailed to write up the show. Adams' temporary quarters were in a basement on Clay Street where the grizzlies and a dog, Rambler, had freedom of the place, and where Mr. Hittell saw Adams repeatedly ride "bear back." The young reporter and the old hunter became firm friends, and a unique and interesting book grew out of their collaboration.

W. K. Fisher.

Index